LETTERS TO
GROWING PAINS

Phillip Hodson is Britain's best-known agony uncle. He appears regularly on BBC1 and TVS programmes and has his own phone-in problem programme on LBC radio each afternoon. He is also the agony uncle for British Telecom (on 0898 12 10 60). Phillip is a fully qualified counsellor and his previous books include *Men – An investigation into the emotional male* (BBC Books, 1984). He lives in London with one son, two step-sons, fellow-counsellor Anne Hooper, a kitten and a lot of old electric trains.

For my Mum (1911–1987)

Please could you help
I am so embarrassed
swimming because I
got spots on my chest
back.

Dear Agony Mister,
           I admit it's
My bedroom is a really bad
BUT I LIKE IT LIKE THAT.
We all get on well at home

I was really pleased to hear
you will be discussing shyne
Growing Pains' this Saturday
suffer from being shy and
me feel really miserable bec
can't be myself when I'm wi
people. I find BLUSHING a
problem. I am so self-consc
if anyone starts talking to
start to blush. I keep th
everybody's watching me all
time. I have seen advertis

Dear Growing Pains
           I am 12 yea
old and madly in love. He
5 foot 10, very handsome
popular. Although he is i
same year as me, I de
know him very well. He's
different from the rest a

LETTERS TO GROWING PAINS

PHILLIP HODSON

Bad Breath. It is a very shameful
problem and I find that I'm unable
to speak to anyone face to face and

Please help. I am 13 and I have got a
lisp. I cannot pronounce words with
the letter 's' in them. I can put up
with it when I'm with people I know
but when I'm walking
street talking to a
some boys or girls s
at me, it really ge

I couldn't possi
with a girl bec
is triangular-s
14 and I shou

Dear Phillip,
I hate my body. I think I'm
too fat. My friends and family
all say that I'm fine but
I know that I'm not. My
Mum and Dad get tired of
me going on at them, and

BBC BOOKS

he problem I have is frie
t all started when my
riend made friends with
ully. The bully, who is

CKNOWLEDGEMENTS

To Cathy Gilbey, Chris Bellinger, Anna Home and
all at the Beeb, especially Sarah Greene for being so kind.
To my son Alexander for helping with the typing and the
rest of the family for living with my deadlines. To Penny
Plain Ltd for my *Growing Pains* sweaters. Special thanks
to all who wrote to *Growing Pains*. This is your book.

Published by BBC Books
A division of BBC Enterprises Ltd
Woodlands, 80 Wood Lane
LONDON W12 0TT

First published 1988

© Phillip Hodson 1988

Typeset in Times and Helvetica
by Wilmaset, Birkenhead, Wirral
Printed and bound in Great Britain by
Richard Clay Ltd, Bungay, Suffolk

ISBN 0563 20635 7

CONTENTS

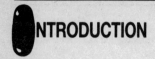

INTRODUCTION

This is a book of some of the letters sent to BBC1's *Saturday Superstore* programme, now called *Going Live*. I've written it because we could never possibly answer on TV everything that you've asked about – not even if the programme started at breakfast and went on till bedtime. I've also written it because nobody seems to bother too much about the real problems and questions of young people up to 14. Parents are pretty good at missing the point sometimes. They mean well when they say 'You'll grow out of it' or 'Don't worry. When you're 20, things will be fine.' But you have this growing pain *now* and the fact that your spots will have vanished when you're old and 21 doesn't solve the problem of being spotty and hating it today. It's funny really. Parents take these 'long-term views' even though they're running out of time themselves. My third reason for doing the book is that sometimes the only information you can get comes from people like me. I'm thinking of the letter from a girl whose periods had just started but her Mum would not or could not tell her about what was happening. Somebody has to help her and I'm happy to try.

Saturday Superstore is now called *Going Live* but my spot, *Growing Pains*, is still there – so if you have a problem and you want to write, the address is simply *Growing Pains*, BBC TV, London W12 8QT. I think we could publish a second volume of these letters next year even if you do address me as 'Dear Acne Uncle'!!

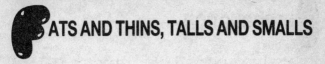ATS AND THINS, TALLS AND SMALLS

FATS

Eating is what a lot of people do when they are not doing anything else. Perhaps you're munching something while you are reading this page? A lot of people have weight problems because they eat to cheer themselves up, to stop worrying or to calm down. Unfortunately this *works* – but only for a short time. As soon as the extra weight appears, you become upset about that as well. I probably get more letters about being too fat than about anything else. It's not surprising when you think how nice it is to eat biscuits, chocolate, cake, chips, jam and sweets, and drink lemonade, cola and hot milk with tons of sugar in it. I like all these things too but they don't like me. They probably make you fat as well. Four out of ten people in Britain *are too heavy*, and there are lots more on the way.

Kathy from Cornwall says she's 13 and simply cannot stick to a diet. Rosie from South Yorkshire is 14 and weighs 9 stone 8 pounds. 'I think I am overweight. I've got a 37-inch bust, 27-inch waist and 38½-inch hips.' She says:

Could you please help? I go swimming every dinnertime and do some running. I also do an exercise tape three times a week. I have tried diets but none of them worked. I have tried the Micro Diet, the Cambridge Diet and many others, but I didn't lose weight with any of them.

Alexandra from Wiltshire writes:

Dear Phillip,
I hate my body. I think I'm too fat. My friends and family all say that I'm fine but I know that I'm not. My Mum and Dad get tired of me going on at them, and they won't let me go on a diet or anything. What can I do to persuade them? Also, I am not very fit. I get out of breath easily.
Please help.
Alexandra

Kathryn from Denbigh says:

I'm overweight and shy and scared of going to school because of it. I go bright red if I have to read in class. I start to stutter and miss out words and I end up making a mess of the whole thing. I get nervous even at the thought of PE and games because of my weight. I have cut out all sweets and cakes and I drink black coffee but I never seem to lose weight. I am 13 years old and all my Mum's friends say I'm very pretty and that I have beautiful hair and skin but I can't see it. My *only* ambition is to lose weight.

Someone just calling himself Boy (and a Sarah Greene fan) mentions the problem of finding clothes to fit:

I'm 14 and quite a bit too heavy. The main drawback for me is the problem of getting affordable fashion clothes for boys. I've been to the doctor but he just gives me diet sheets and they are hard to stick to. I would try that new acid tablet that eats away fat but they're for adults only . . .

Hazel from Bingley agrees:

I'm a size 16 to 18 so clothes are hard to find. My school blouses are a tight fit and school blouses only go up to a 40-inch bust (I'm just over). I weigh 12 stone and I'm 5 foot 5 inches tall.

Zöe from Carshalton says:

I have a weight problem around my bum, hips and legs.
I've tried doing exercises and swimming but it doesn't
seem to have done any good. I'm 14 years old and
around 5 foot 3 or 4 inches. All my friends have nice
figures, eat what they like and don't seem to put on any
weight. This just makes me feel worse. I'm desperate for
some advice.

Anonymous in Sheffield complains about Mum:

When I talk to my Mum she just says that we will go on a
diet but when it comes round to it she always forgets and
buys silly food. Not only is my stomach fat but I also have
a massive bottom and thighs. At school, no one ever
picks me for their team.

V from Twyford has bought an exercise bike:

I use it morning and evening at 30 mph for 5 miles. It
doesn't seem to work . . .

Sonya from Oxford says:

I am scared to go in the school showers because
everyone makes fun of my wobbles.

Paula from Sunbury complains:

I am 10 years old and 7 stone. My Mum's boyfriend calls
me 'fatty'. He also calls me 'pong ferret'.

Another Anonymous raises the question of boyfriends:

I am 13, and 9½ stone. Having such a weight problem is
preventing boys from going out with me. I am the only girl
in my class who hasn't had a boyfriend in the last year and
it gets depressing because I don't get invited to discos.
My Mum thinks it has to do with my being a vegetarian.

Julie from Warwick says:

Weight is a problem that causes me a lot of worry and stress. I weigh just under 10 stone (at 14¾ years old) and I am plump. Being overweight can really make me depressed at times, especially when everywhere you go you are surrounded by the image of the 'perfect woman', who is tall and slim and pretty. When I look at a magazine or newspaper and see slim, perfect women, it makes me feel even worse about myself and the way I look. I confess I do eat a lot. It's easy for people to say 'don't eat this' and 'don't eat that' and go on all sorts of diets, but it isn't easy at all – it takes an awful lot of willpower. I walk a lot each day and do as much exercise as I can when I get home. Though I feel a lot better about myself after exercising, I don't seem to lose that much weight. Is it possible to lose weight by exercising a lot? And is being overweight an inherited thing?

Amanda from Mexborough has the problem very badly:

I am 15 years old and the problem is that I weigh 21 stone. It is making me very depressed. I have no friends, no hope of a job and no money, and all I do is sit around watching television all day and eating . . .

Amanda is in real trouble. I don't think it's just that getting fat has made her depressed. I think the *illness* of depression has made her fat. When people are very unhappy, they sometimes just eat and eat and eat, non-stop. I once had to try and help a little boy of 7 who had *doubled* in size in the weeks after his mother died. Getting depressed is not your fault. Sometimes, eating seems to be the only way to try and cope. But Amanda should definitely see the doctor to be checked for other problems that might be contributing to the weight-gain and to get help with her depression. As I see it, she feels empty. Her life is empty. There is nothing good to look forward to. And when we feel that hollow inside, we try to stuff ourselves simply to feel a bit more 'solid'. A diet sheet by itself is not going to help.

About one third of the population is 10 per cent overweight because they take in more energy (in the form of food) than they use up. Dieting is useless in the short term – you usually just get rid of water and something called glycogen (not fat) – even if you starve for a month. Then, when you eat, the glycogen and the water are replaced and you end up weighing the same.

To shift fat successfully, you have to eat less for good, and take some exercise for good. You must change your lifestyle. You have to plan your campaign over the year rather than the week or just a couple of days. (The *Going Live* producer went on a diet on a Friday and asked her family if they could tell by Saturday lunchtime. PS – This is a joke!)

I also know how miserable it feels to be fat. When I was 7 I was 7 stone. When I was 14 I was 14 stone but when I was 17 I was 11 stone. I hated stripping on the beach on holiday. I hated not being able to 'get' anybody in the playground when they teased me and I hated not being able to run in the school cross-country. The annual race (in front of all the girls) was about three miles long but I could only make it from the starting line to the first road – after that I had to walk. I thought I would never lose weight, but I did. Here are some tips that I found useful – perhaps you will too:

- Don't fool yourself that being fat makes you a terrible person.

- Eat a good, balanced diet with less meat, almost no sugar, very little butter, more fruit and vegetables than before, but *don't* cut bulk. A diet won't work if you're hungry. If you're hungry, you get obsessed with eating. I enjoyed baked potatoes which fill you up but are low in calories, provided you don't smother them with cheese and butter.

- Eat more slowly, really tasting the food. Don't snack on chocolate or salty foods because they are too *exciting* and make you want more. For example, those who eat a choc before a meal or between courses have been shown to eat an average 478 calories *more* during the meal. It helps to have a food routine – especially a rather boring one. So don't put sugar in savoury meals either. In other words, lay off the sauces and pickles.

- Make exercise a part of your life forever. Choose your favourite (or least unfavourite) sport or activity. Your body is built to carry you around. Your legs were designed to walk *all day* if necessary. If you sit in buses or cars, don't blame the world if you get fatter. The food you eat is supposed to provide the energy to make you move under your own power. For instance, since Kathy from Cornwall wrote to me she has taken up synchronised swimming and has slowly but surely lost weight over the past 11 months.

- Try to teach yourself new habits of mind. If your parents have always bribed you with pudding to eat up your brussel sprouts, tell yourself it will be different from now on. You will not binge. You will eat enough of everything to keep you energetic between meals. The best way to do that is to have some first course and a little fruit or a small portion of something sweet for afters. No eating between meals. Ask for smaller portions *before* the meal is cooked so parents don't get taken by surprise.

It helps if you plan your progress with a chart over the year. Make it 'The Year of the Diet'. But don't be too much of a perfectionist. One slip into a packet of potato crisps doesn't mean you abandon your diet. Just forgive yourself. Always be pleased with the positive. Say 'I lost 2 pounds this month. Hooray it's working!' rather than 'I only lost 2 pounds this month, it isn't working!'

If your parents find it ultra-difficult to let you eat sensibly (always loading up your plate or forcing you to eat what you hate), then maybe you have to show them that you are growing up faster than they imagine in other ways too. Perhaps you could help more with the shopping. Perhaps you could do a few more jobs around the house. If you helped *prepare* some of the meals, it would be easier to suggest what they should contain and who should have a tomato instead of fried rice or chips with the fish fingers. (There is no evidence to show that vegetarians get fatter than meat-eaters, by the way.) Remember, your parents cannot stop you taking exercise. When you do, you will burn up more energy, and you tend not to binge when your system is fully fit.

Helen from Gosport has these words of encouragement for all dieters:

I have a weight problem but I want to offer my support to anybody else who has the same problem. My friends have been very good to me. They don't offer me sweets but at the end of every month, my best friend buys me a Mars Bar if I have lost more than 2 pounds, and my weight is gradually going down. Also, if by the end of Easter I have reduced to 8½ stone, my Mum is going to let me have my ears pierced. My message is DON'T GIVE UP! Good luck.

Rewards for achieving your targets can be helpful although I think a Mars Bar is perhaps *not* the very best prize when the goal is weight loss. Possibly, your best friend could be persuaded to take you to the cinema, or buy you a record instead, although if the system works, it works.

Marjorie from Edinburgh (now grown up) has words of warning for young dieters:

After hearing your new problem spot *Growing Pains*, I decided to tell you about my trouble which began when I was only 13.

You see, I developed the slimmer's disease anorexia nervosa. Eight years later, I still cannot eat normally. I am either fasting or bingeing. Sometimes I wonder when it will all end. When I am slim, I feel on top of the world. But when I have been bingeing, I feel totally depressed and disgusted with myself.

I think the reason my illness has gone on for so long is that I never got any real help. Nobody tried to understand why I was starving myself. I didn't even know why I was doing it. If the root of my problem had been revealed, I now feel it would have helped me to recover totally.

Many people get angry with anorexics, which only makes them worse. All we need is someone to try and understand our fear of getting fat.

But one thing I do remember about my illness was that I thought about becoming thin all the time. I truly believed that this would mean having more friends, being successful, popular and more attractive. Yet, ironically, everything went the opposite way.

I am writing this letter to warn young girls about extreme dieting. Dieting is safe as long as you stick to 1000 calories a day. Please be sensible about losing weight. Do not crash-diet.

Anorexia is a disabling disease. It prevents you from mixing with people or going anywhere where food may be on the table. I still cannot plan things too far ahead as I don't know if I'll be fasting or bingeing that week.

It has made me a very sad and lonely person. I cannot talk about it to anybody. That's why I wrote this letter.

Anorexia is not just about slimming too much. The real trouble is feeling unable to express yourself and talk about your problems, perhaps because nobody will let you or listen to you. Giving up food is part of a battle to get taken more seriously as a person, although your parents may find it impossible to understand that. There is also the thought that needy, greedy, 'fat' people will never be accepted by others. However, liking yourself, enjoying your food and even becoming plump are *not* the same as being horrid or nasty or evil. If you would like to talk to someone about anorexia or bulimia (bingeing), then contact Anorexic Aid, The Priory Centre, 11 Priory Road, High Wycombe, Buckinghamshire HP13 6SL (telephone – 0494 21431). Penguin Books have also published a book about anorexia called *Catherine*. It's written by Maureen Dunbar and helps explain an illness that even doctors find hard to understand.

Finally on fat, let's hear from a Mum who is proud of her daughter for dieting the right way:

I regularly watch *Growing Pains*, your spot on teenage problems, with great admiration and enjoyment.

I would like to tell you about one of my children, my

daughter Debbie who is 16 years old (now). She used to have a weight problem which caused me concern too, as it was starting to affect her in every way (e.g. bullying at school, embarrassing remarks, etc.). Although Debbie could take care of herself, it was beginning to wear her down.

Just over a year ago, Debbie decided that the time had come to do something about her problem, so with great determination and courage, she commenced her campaign which consisted of a calorie-controlled diet, keep fit (in the privacy of her bedroom), jogging and, after a time, socialising at a local youth club.

It has been a long, hard struggle but she has gone from a size 18 to a size 12 to 14. I am so proud of her.

I work with young people, many of whom are very conscious of their figures (not just their weight) and I have quoted Debbie's success story to several of them, as I felt they were going about dieting the wrong way, to the point of almost starving themselves.

We'll see why it's so important to feel comfortable with your appearance at the end of this chapter. But first, I want to look at things through the other end of the telescope.

THINS

You see, the big surprise for Kathy, Rosie, Alexandra, Kathryn, Boy, Hazel, Zöe, V, Sonya, Paula and Julie, is that they are envied by tons of people of their own age who are desperate to *gain* weight. For instance, listen to Ellie:

Today on *Going Live* I heard lots of people complaining that they were overweight. Well they should put themselves in my shoes. I'm almost 15, 5 foot 9 inches tall and weigh just over $7\frac{1}{2}$ stone. I am very tall and very thin. I eat lots of food (the right kind). I'm on a high-fibre diet. I'm not a very athletic person.

I hate it when people complain about being overweight and wish they were thin. It's not worth it. I get picked on at school. I can never find clothes that fit and I always feel weak. I WOULD RATHER BE FAT THAN THIN ANY DAY. I'm sure there are lots of people in my state but I've never heard of a 'get fat diet'. Nobody bothers with them because people think it's nice to be thin, but it's not. I am always getting asked if I'm anorexic.

I HATE IT! WHY DOESN'T ANYBODY CATER FOR PEOPLE WHO WANT TO GET FAT AND CAN'T?

Some nights I cry myself to sleep because of people always complaining that they're overweight and want to look like me. But I would never wish that on anyone.

Mona from Birmingham has a similar problem:

Dear Uncle Agony,

I am writing to you because I think you can help me. I have a weight problem. No! I'm not fat but the opposite – skinny. That is my problem and I don't know what to do about it. When I was 12 years old, I used to weigh 5 stone 2 pounds. Now that I am 15 and will soon be 16, I only weigh 6 stone 3 pounds. I'm getting very worried. When I was a newborn baby I weighed 8 pounds 7 ounces and I was healthy and cute. I don't know what's gone wrong. I am developing properly. I've taken tonics and vitamin pills but they don't seem to have any effect on me. The doctor says she can prescribe medicine and that's all. Oh! Please help me. I eat a lot but it doesn't seem to help.

Angie from the Borders feels the same way:

Dear Mr Agony,

I have a problem. I am very thin. I have knobbly knees and my bones stick out in all the worst places. People at school make fun of me and I get picked on. Another problem is that my veins stick out on my hands and feet. I love sport but am very embarrassed about wearing shorts or a short skirt. The rest of the time I wear baggy trousers or very long skirts.

I eat a lot and seem to put on weight but there is no evidence of where it goes!

Matchstick from Glasgow also has problems with clothes:

I am writing to you because of my shape, size and weight. I am fairly tall but very thin. Every time I try on skirts or trousers they just drop over my hips and hang round my thighs. My Mum has to take them in about an inch each side.

I am 5 stone. I get teased by the boys who call me 'stick insect'. It's not just the teasing that gets to me. It's the way people think they can push me around because I have a slight disadvantage. So what do I do? Stick a pillow up my jumper? Or wear boxing gloves with weights in them?

And then there's Anonymous of North Wales:

SOS please. I need some advice about putting on weight. You always hear of people wanting to lose weight but we skinny people feel just as desperate. I'm nearly 14 and 5 foot 3 inches in height.

There seems to be no reason why I'm thin, as I've had all the normal medical tests. But that still doesn't help me with my problem. My legs are painfully thin and they can only be hidden by trousers which I wear all year through. I'm going abroad soon and would dearly love to wear a swimsuit. Please can you advise me on how to put on at least another stone?

Finally Carrie from Exeter says:

I'm writing to tell you about my shape. I'm thin and people

at school call me 'skinny ribs'. They also call me
'waterworks' because I cry a lot when I'm picked on and
bullied. I've got one friend called Mary. But sometimes
she's one of them as well. What can I do?
From Carrie, aged 9

From these letters, it is clear that there are some
advantages to being plump. However, there are
also some advantages to being thinner:

● You are probably healthier in some ways, even
  though you haven't got a 'reserve of fat' to tide
  you through an illness. You are putting less stress
  on your heart, and your joints are not likely to
  get so worn down by carrying your body weight.
● It may seem difficult to find fashionable clothes,
  and you may feel awkward about going
  swimming, but long clothes will hang well on
  you. Remember, we all tend to put on weight as
  we get older so your problem may get better with
  time and this is not so true of fatter people.
● You don't have to worry about eating too many
  fattening foods!

However, the plain fact is that gaining weight is
harder than losing it. Some people have a fast
metabolism, meaning that their bodies process food
quickly, so even if they eat and eat they do not put
on weight. But there is a special diet available (send
a stamped addressed envelope to Michael Van
Straten, PO Box 261, London EC4P 4LP, asking
for the Weight Gain Diet sheet). You have to
concentrate a bit on food, never skipping a meal.
You could try some body-building exercises for
particular groups of muscles if you wish. Undoub-
tedly a high-protein diet will help you gain some
muscle tissue. But don't make being thin into a

major catastrophe. Just because you are thin, it doesn't mean that your life is a mess. It is something you'll be aware of from time to time but it is no reason to believe that people can always put you down. You haven't got a thin voice, for example, so you are still able to make your views and opinions clearly heard.

TALLS

Body size is not simply a matter of how wide you are. There's also the vexed issue of feeling that you are too tall, as with Sarah of Bromley:

Dear *Growing Pains*,
I'm 5 foot 4 and I'm 11 years old. I used to be the same size as my friends but now I tower over them. When people visit they say 'Gosh, isn't she tall?'
   I HATE IT.
   Friends at school say I'm taking tablets to make me tall. I also have a problem with my weight. I'm 8 stone, but I'm not fat.
   I have a big bust too. At games, they laugh at me and say I should wear a bra. I do wear one, but not at games because they would laugh at me even more. I've tried.
PLEASE HELP ME.

Then there's S from Swindon who suffers from feeling 'stretched':

I am a 14-year-old girl who is nearly 5 foot 9 inches tall. As you can well imagine, I have long legs. This leads to a very embarrassing problem. I have quite noticeable stretch marks at the tops of my legs.
   My Mum says they will fade as I grow older, but I get teased very badly by other girls at my school.

And 'The Dinosaur', also female:

I get more and more worried that I will never have a boyfriend. Nobody in their right mind would want a 6-foot tall, 13-stone giant like me. I dwarf anyone who comes near me. What is worse is that because of my size I am forced into wearing clothes that I hate. Have you ever tried getting a decent pair of trousers in a size 18? All those baggy-style clothes are skin-tight on me.

There are a few shops for big sizes but there is nothing worse than seeing a 60-year-old woman buying the same clothes as you. They make bigger clothes but not bigger fashion clothes. I can't even wear jeans anymore.

Now imagine me – tall, well-built and totally square. I must disgust all the males.

People say it's what's inside you that counts but how will anyone get to know me if I repel them so much?

I am almost 15 and I have never been out with anyone. My best friend tells me that my time will come (she's been out with five boys since she was 11), but I'm not so sure.
Sincerely,
The Dinosaur (my nickname)

The next letter is from Anonymous:

Dear Mr Claire Rayner (?!),
My problem is that I am tall (5 foot 5 inches). I can't even walk through the school gate without people staring at me and calling me names, and I'm getting sick of it. I try to ignore the names, but it doesn't work and I end up getting really depressed. My Mum says I will fill out as I get older but that won't stop people laughing at me now.

Emma of Dagenham wants to know:

When will I stop growing? I am nearly 5 foot 6 inches tall and I always get called 'lanky'. Please tell me when it will stop, since I'm only 12.

Susan of Lanark is 15 but feels the same:

My problem is my height as I am almost 6 foot tall. My Mum says I take after my father but this is not a great deal of help. As you might guess, my height causes great problems because I like a boy who is smaller than me. I am worried that my friends will come out with cutting comments if they see me with him.

Davina from Bath also has problems with friends:

Dear Acne Uncle,
I am 5 foot 8¾ inches tall at 13. All my friends are around 5 foot 4 inches tall. I look really big in comparison. People call me 'lanky' and 'beanpole' and 'clothesprop' but I am not lanky, I am just *tall*. I wouldn't mind being a model but I still think 5 foot 9 inches is too tall for a 13-year-old. Also, I like to wear heels but they make me look even taller.

Carol-Anne from Barnes wants to know what lies in store:

I am only 13 and 5 foot 8 inches tall – and that was the last time I was measured, which was over six months ago.

What I want to ask is: will I keep on growing until I am 18 and, if so, will I grow another couple of inches or more?

I would hate to be 6 foot tall but if you tell me about it now then it will not come unexpectedly.
Worried *Growing Pains* fan

'C' from Berkshire (that's his code name) says:

I am so much taller than everyone else in my class that I tend to crouch down instead of standing up straight. Is this dangerous?

Let's look at the facts of height. When you're in your teens, you want to be like your friends. If you stand out, you get teased. Unfortunately, we don't grow at the same rates and we aren't all going to be the same size (because we come from different sets of parents who are themselves of different sizes). *So we can't have what we want – to be all the same in appearance.*

The average height for British adult women is from 5 foot to 5 foot 10 inches tall (152 cm to 176 cm). The average equivalent for adult men is from 5 foot 4 inches to 6 foot 1 inch tall (163 cm to 186 cm). *If that's the average, it follows that lots of normal people will be a bit shorter or taller than the average.*

That means there will be normal women who are 6 foot tall and normal men who are 6 foot 6 inches tall, or even more.

The real catch is that some people reach their *final adult height* when they're still in their early or mid-teens. So you can never find a class of 14-year-olds who are all the same height. Some boys and girls begin puberty two or three years earlier than others. The only comfort is to tell yourself that if you have already reached the upper adult limits by 13 or 14, then you will probably hardly grow at all after that.

However, a word of caution. If you began shooting up before the age of 9, it's a good idea to have a word with your doctor, or get your parents to take you for a check-up. Or, again, if you find that you keep on growing year after year at a rate that concerns you, with no signs of slowing up, even if your parents are tall, you should discuss this with your GP.

Otherwise, since it's not your fault and you cannot shrink into the ground, it's a good idea to *be* the height that you are. What I mean by that, 'C', is definitely *not* to become round-shouldered for life (which is possible if you hunch yourself up for long enough) but to stand up straight and to deal with any teasing by looking *down* on your tormentors. If you cannot think of anything to say in reply, a slow smile from a height is always very effective, especially if you carry yourself proudly so that others don't feel you are ashamed of being prominent. As a nation, we are in fact getting taller, so the conventional heights are gradually being left behind. And, in this age of equality, so is the idea that the boy must *always* be taller than the girl.

Again, if you think your whole life has been ruined because you are a giant, I suggest this is a way of *not* looking at all the other things that are a problem for you. Why are you so depressed anyway? Why doesn't anybody talk to you about it? Or is it that you won't talk about it to them? Why do you feel alone? Why do you feel everything is so hopeless? You cannot change your height or rush the rate at which your stretch marks fade but there is a lot you can do to change your relationships with parents, teachers, friends and above all *yourself*.

SMALLS

The worries about *not* growing tall enough are just as natural as those we've already discussed. If it's normal for some people to shoot up before others, it's equally normal for those who've been left behind to feel bad about it. As Mansoor from Bradford puts it:

I am 11 years old and I am badly under weight. I weigh just under 4 stone. I am also short for my age. I'm about 4 foot 5 inches tall and I'm very skinny. All my friends at school call me 'titchy' or 'midget'. When they call me that I try to ignore them and laugh, but I'm really hurting inside. I know they are just teasing but I still get upset.

I'm sure you will think I'm stupid if I tell you that I hate it when people call me 'sweet' or 'cute' because I am 11 years old and I go to high school. I do get embarrassed when people do this – it's as though I'm a 4-year-old. I really need advice on how to handle my problem.

SS from Chichester says:

I am 15 years old and short for my age (4 foot 9 inches). I look like an 11-year-old and they tell me I won't grow any more because I have already started my periods. Is there something I can do about my height please!!!!!
(PS – My Mum is short too.)

Keri from Mold is worried about future jobs:

I am 15½ and I am the smallest in my class. What worries me is the fact that my height bars me from so many careers, e.g. the police force, nursing, being an air stewardess, a receptionist in an airport or a firewoman. What happens to those people who are too small to follow the career they want? They have to abandon their dreams! I think this is unfair. Surely height is not that important?

Simon from Finchley makes his point bluntly:

I am only writing a short letter because that is my problem. I am 15 years old and I am the smallest in our third year (out of 360 people) – one of my friends is 6 foot 3 inches tall. I can't get into '15' films at the cinema – my Mum says I'll grow in a couple of years time (although everyone else says I'll be a dwarf!!). In many ways, being small is an advantage but I can't buy any good clothes because they're all too big for me.

And then there's a letter from X of Suffolk, who is really getting into a depression about her size:

Dear Uncle Agony,

I have watched you answer many problems on TV. I just pray that you can help me too. I am 14 and have been crash-dieting for six months to get rid of past plumpness. However my 'midget' height of 4 foot 10 inches causes major problems for me. People don't ever take me seriously, but laugh and mock me without even realising. My friends are all above average height (5 foot 4 inches) and when I go with them I am pushed to the back and neglected. I am constantly questioned about my age in cinemas and on buses. People in the street treat me as a child. Sometimes I feel so much less of a person and such a disappointment to my family that I sit for whole days in my bedroom crying and imagining I'm someone else – anyone in fact but me. Sometimes I even pray I may get run over by a car on the way to school or find out that I have some incurable disease which explains my height. When someone calls me something or my friends say in conversation 'Oh X would know about Mothercare' I want to go to sleep and never wake up. Please help me, I am desperate. Is there any address I can write to, to obtain information?

Well, X, you seem to assume you've stopped growing but this is almost certainly not true. You're also not doing justice to your real problems. As I see it, you will inevitably get angry when people think you're younger than you are and challenge your right to watch certain films. But you are overlooking how bad you feel about separate matters:

○ the fact is you are depressed
○ the fact is you are shy

○ the fact is you are lonely
○ the fact is you seem a bit miserable about your family
○ the fact is you can even wonder whether your Mum and Dad don't care for you because you are not taller.

You cannot deal with these problems unless you identify them correctly instead of only focusing on your size. It might help for instance if you let your parents know that you feel so gloomy about your life so that they could be more affectionate and supportive. If you felt you belonged more, you'd feel bigger inside right away.

And anybody else who feels they're not growing fast enough can get information on normal rates of growth from a helpful group called The Child Growth Foundation, 2 Mayfield Avenue, Chiswick, London W4 1PW. But bear in mind that human growth is usually not completed until you are about 18 and that there is a normal range of 10 inches between the shortest and tallest teenage girl, and 9 inches between the shortest and tallest teenage boy (and the same for adults). Your final height depends on family factors. For instance, if you're a boy with a Dad of 6 foot 3 inches and a Mum of 5 foot 2 inches, you will probably grow up to be shorter than your Dad but taller than your Mum. Practically no boy is shorter than his Mum and the average final height increase over her is about 5 or 6 inches. If you're a girl with parents of this sort of height, you will probably grow up to be on average some 3 to 4 inches shorter than the boy. Tall parents will mostly have tall children. Short short. If a short man marries a tall woman, their children are likely to be taller than him. While it is true that the main 'growth spurt' for girls comes to an end when their periods start (on average at 13 years 3 months), growing can continue for some time after that. If it didn't, we'd have a nation of women no taller than the majority of 13-year-old girls. The growth spurt for boys lasts until they are over 16.

A word of caution. If you are undersized and worried about it, by all means make a visit to your doctor since if there is a medical reason for lack of growth this can *only* be put right while you are still young enough to be 'able' to grow. If you are told there is nothing at all wrong with you physically, then I'm afraid nothing whatever can be done to make you taller – however unfair life may seem. The only way in which you can 'grow' in these circumstances is from the inside, in your *attitudes*.

Just make up your mind that, however tiny your frame may be, you can still be a *big person*. Don't make size an excuse to accept being pushed around by others. Here are a few tips you could try:

● Speak in a louder voice than normal, slowing down your speech and saying every word clearly and forcefully. One of my friends, Brian Hayes, works on the radio. He is quite small but nobody can ever ignore him because he always speaks up for himself. It is impossible to overlook him!
● Always look people in the eye when you start to talk to them. I don't mean that you should bore them to death with your menacing stare. Occasionally, it is normal to glance away while chatting. But by making 'eye contact' you show you are neither afraid of them nor unfriendly.
● Smile when you meet people. It will make them think you feel confident – and that is what you are trying to achieve, isn't it?

We don't like being too *fat* or *thin* or *tall* or *small* because our bodies are part of our *identity*. They are what other people see first. We imagine that other people see us as we see ourselves but that is impossible. (They're more worried about themselves anyway.) So when we get teased, we think we are being told the absolute truth about ourselves instead of seeing that it's just an attempt to upset us. If we don't bite, they will get bored. And if we look at ourselves in the mirror we can always find the good bits. No one is entitled to look perfect and no one does. So find your best feature and tell yourself how pretty your nose or smile or hair is, whenever anybody says you look too fat or thin or tall or small. We are not made in factories. We all come from different families of differently sized people.

CHAPTER 2

FAMILY RULES AND ROWS

One thing I say on television is that children sometimes need to educate their parents. This is not meant to sound anti-grown-up. After all, I am a parent myself and don't take kindly to being pushed around. What I mean is that it is often difficult for parents with busy lives to stay in touch with the rate at which children grow up. They may not know what is 'normal' for your age group – how late you should stay out, what time you should be going to bed, how much homework you have to do, how many of your friends have already been out with a boy or girl of the opposite sex. Things like that. They may also not notice that you can look after yourself more than they find comfortable. You see, being a parent is a job and some people really like it! Mums and Dads sometimes find it very difficult to lose this job. It may mean they have to find something else to do. They could even find that there is nothing else they want to do, and that's really tough. So that's one reason why they go on treating you like a kid when you're not. They hate change.

Educating your parents means showing them, by behaving in an adult way, that you are ready for a bit more freedom than they realised. They are only going to treat you in a grown-up fashion if you:

○ learn to negotiate
○ don't just make angry demands

○ don't sulk
○ give them reasons for your viewpoint
○ show that you have researched the problem.
  (Maybe show them some of the letters in this
  book for comparison.)

So when your Dad is shouting at you (i.e.
behaving like a child) because you want to go to the
fair till 10.30 at night, show him that you have
thought about how to get there safely, how to get
back, how to pay for it and why a treat is due. Say
all this in a nice, steady voice – and you will soon
make him feel that *he's* the one being unreason-
able. My son does this to me often and I have to
report that it works . . .
Naturally, your parents remain in charge of you
and responsible for you. You are living in their
home and they have the right to make the basic
rules. There will never be complete agreement in
the family on how to live, so you'll have to expect
some conflict. A sensible person will say, 'Since this
cannot be avoided, I will attempt to reach com-
promises giving me *enough* of what I want.'

Bella in Northampton needs to do this:

I am 13 and I am writing to you because whenever I sit
down to a meal my mother moans as I eat. She says
things like 'Oh you pig' and 'Shut your mouth when you
eat' and 'Why don't you just shovel it in at once, then you
won't have to keep moving your hand up and down?' And
if I cough sometimes she says 'Got some food stuck in
your throat – unchewed food often gets stuck, you know!'
This annoys me to pieces, but I must admit I do eat like a
pig and I'm very fat. What can I do to stop this agonising
mother?

Well, my answer to that is to offer a deal – 'I'll stop eating like a pig, as you put it, if you'll stop talking about my eating.' You're clearly in a power struggle with your Mum anyway and I guess you enjoy winding her up a bit. The problem is that you also pay for it. She gets wound up and nags you back. You're winning by reducing her to helpless moaning but losing by wasting time, getting fat (gobbling makes you overweight by confusing your appetite) and putting people's backs up. Can you feel 'important' in a more constructive way, perhaps by doing something useful for the family? For instance, what about walking the dog regularly? That would be good for your figure too.

Then there's Joanna in Bowmansgreen:

Dear Phillip,
I have a very bad problem with my Mum. I'm always getting told off because I am a very very fussy eater. I hardly eat anything – please help me. I don't eat any greens or vegetables. I hope you can help.
Yours sincerely,
Joanna, aged 10

So what you're saying, Joanna, is that you're fed up with being so picky about food. The remedy is in your own hands – it's called a knife and fork. We all like different amounts of food but I think you are using food to express the kind of worry which it might be more useful to *talk* about. At the moment, you overlook the joy, fun and *power* of tasting new experiences. I offer you my 'vegetable' challenge.

Since what you really want is to feel more powerful, why not get the feeling this way? Choose a vegetable you don't positively hate. Next time they're served up, ask for three big ones, eat them up and *see* if you survive. Your parents will be astonished and you will have turned the tables on them. Think about it. Wouldn't you like to be so much in control of your actions and their reactions? Be honest? Try it and see. (PS – This is not a trick to get at you. I'm only asking you to do it once to see what happens. And if you like the feeling – continue.)

Tim in Kidderminster has the bedtime blues:

Dear Mr Agony,
I am writing to you because I have a problem. My mother and father say that I have to go to bed at 8.30. Sometimes my friends ask, 'Did you watch that good film at about 9.30 last night?' It's really embarrassing to say, 'No, I was in bed at that time.'
   What time do *you* think a 13/14-year-old should go to bed? Also, many of my best programmes are on late, so I miss a lot of them. So how do I get to stay up a bit later?

Well, I suggest you tell them that you know they have good reasons for wanting you to go to bed early. But you find that you don't need quite as much sleep as before (unless, of course, you do a paper round and get up at 4 am). Different people sleep for different lengths of time at different ages. The Prime Minister says she does well on 5 hours a night. My 8-year-old son does not need to sleep till 9 or 9.30 and he's still up at 7 the next morning (darn it!).
   Find out what time all the kids in your class go to bed and tell your parents the average time, rather than putting too much emphasis on your real grouse about the television. Parents think homework is very important, so your case will be stronger if you agree to do this at the start of the evening. If it's something your family can really afford, see what

the chances are of obtaining a video. Forty per cent of British homes now have one, if that's a useful argument for you to use.

Lots of your letters ask about dating, like this one from Marjorie in Tooting:

I would like to ask your advice on how to tell my parents that I have got a boyfriend. He is 13, the same age as me, and he has told me that his parents know he is seeing me and they don't mind. So I thought it was about time my parents got to know about it. As I have been seeing him for about two weeks, I am scared about how my parents will react and worried that they'll ask me why I didn't tell them sooner.

And this one from Maddy in Leatherhead:

Please tell me what to do. There is a boy in my school who I would like to go out with. He is 15 and I am 13 but my mother won't let me go out with boys. She says I am too young and if she found out she would kill me.

  I keep telling her that there are girls of 10 going out with boys but she doesn't listen. Also, the boy I want to go out with would expect me to stay out till about 10 o'clock at night. I am so worried and don't think about anything else.

Martin from Reading says:

I will be 15 in a few days' time and both my parents still refuse to allow me to go out with girls. I have tried every logical argument I can think of but they still insist that I am too young. Do you think that they are being unreasonably protective?

  It's getting to the point where I'm considering doing something behind their backs. I don't want to do this, but if things go on the way they are, I might have to. What would you advise me to do?

And then there are rows about when you should come home if you *are* allowed out on a date or to a disco. This letter comes from Earl in Wakefield:

I have a nice Mum and Dad but we have arguments about what time I should come in at night.

I like to go out with my mates. We just hang about and chat and go to a coffee bar or someone's house to play records. We're not doing anything wrong but my parents always want to *know* where I am going and who I am going with, and if we change our minds I'm supposed to phone up and tell them.

It makes me feel like a baby. None of my friends have to do this.

How can I make them understand that I know what I am doing and I won't ever do anything silly?

They also say I have to be in by 10 pm and I'm 14 years old.

They don't like my clothes either – they want me to look really old-fashioned. How can I get them to listen to me?

Derek in Liverpool complains:

My parents never let me go to parties and they never let me stay over at my friend's house. I even have to be in by 10 pm. I never question them – do you think I should be more rebellious? I'm now 16.

I think the way to handle all these problems is by preparing a case which you present to your parents. If you need to tell them you have a special friend, it's obviously a help if you can say his or her parents already know about it and approve, and ask if they would like to meet them. If your Mum says you are not allowed to have a boyfriend, then ask all the follow-up questions: how long is the ban to last? Will you be 18 before she relents? If not 18, then 17? Or 16? Or possibly 15? And does she mean having *no* male friends round to the family home? Or is that all right? Telling her that girls of 10 are going steady cuts no ice. She simply disapproves. Telling her that most girls of your age *occasionally* go out with someone might work. If she shifts her position a bit, you must shift yours. Whatever time your bloke-to-be 'insists' you have to stay out till (who's he to 'insist', anyway?), agree with her in advance when you will come home.

When parents seem too protective, you should try to get them to voice their anxieties about you. It will do them good. Show that you have heard what they say and are grateful they care about you. Say it would be nice if they made it clear that they didn't disapprove of you and your mates. This will do you good. Ask them when they think the rules might be changed and whether any minor rules can be altered now. If they insist that you cannot have a girlfriend or boyfriend at all, find out their reasons and see if you can meet their objections halfway by changes in your own behaviour. Start your campaign by going out in a group of both sexes, to which they may not object, and work from there.

Ella in Hereford has a different concern:

Dear Mr *Growing Pains*,
I am 15 going on 16 and I have a younger sister. I am writing to you because nobody will see my point of view.

My problem is that my sister goes into my bedroom when I'm not there and snoops around. I have asked for a lock to be put on my door but everyone thinks I'm being silly about the whole thing. I like to keep my personal secrets somewhere where they can remain my personal secrets, but no matter where I hide them my sister always finds them and then I get embarrassed. Do you think I am old enough and should have a lock? Or do you think I am being silly as well?

I'll tell you what, I like to keep my personal secrets 'secret' too. Most of us do. Your sister wants to ferret them out because she feels they are secrets held against her, and perhaps some of them are. She resents you for being older, more grown-up and the first-born. Therefore you need to protect your privacy. Maybe your parents don't want you to have a lock on your bedroom door in case there is a fire and they can't get in. Why not ask for a lockable box for Christmas? They're easy to make and they do keep small sisters out.

Daphne in Birmingham also has trouble with secrets:

I'm 16 and my boyfriend is 17 – the problem is his Mum. She once found some letters I'd sent him and she read them. Now she knows everything that has gone on between us. The situation is unbearable, as she has demanded that he stop seeing me. Sometimes I feel suicidal because I can't bear life without him. What can we do about it? I haven't seen his parents since the incident and mine don't know.

It would be best to tell your parents about your difficulty and perhaps approach your boyfriend's family with them. What you are really playing for is *time*. If you could get permission to resume the relationship, maybe on a less 'passionate' basis (I do not know exactly what has happened), his mother might come round a bit. In a couple of years, you will be in charge of your own lives anyway.

Abby in Doncaster is fed up with her family:

I don't get on at all well with my Mum and all we do is argue and bitch about each other.

It started about four months ago when my brother got a modelling job. Mum has always preferred my brother to my sister or me! She never picks on my sister who is mentally handicapped, so the only one left to pick on is me.

About five months ago, I made friends with a girl at school and we became best friends. I used to go home after school and greet my mother with a smile and I used to be met with an argument. When my brother (who is 10) got home, I'd be completely ignored in favour of him. My Dad never gave me any reason to be upset. He's a saint – I really love him. Eventually, I couldn't stand it any longer so my friend and her Mum said I could stay at their house. I went there for a week non-stop without going home at all – just seeing my Dad at work to get my dinner money. Now I'm home again and things are just as bad. Please help.

It seems to me that your Mum is under a lot of stress (perhaps because of coping with your sister?) and you might sit down and ask yourself what that does to people? Does it make them ratty? Will they unfairly expect more of those members of the family who are not handicapped? Will it make them look for a scapegoat sometimes? In other words, you're in a line of fire and the problem is how to move out of it.

Perhaps your father has a little more time and energy to listen to your troubles and give you some extra attention. Perhaps there could be a family 'sit-down' where you simply said the rows were making you feel rotten, asked what your Mum really expected of you and stated, in return, what you'd like from her. Could you offer her some sort of deal for the future and could she possibly admit she sometimes says things to you that she does not mean? Try it.

Bev in Solihull is bothered by Sundays:

My father is a Catholic and enjoys taking me to church every week. I find it very boring and I don't understand many of the words because I am only 12 so I just sit there. My sister stopped going when she was 15 but I can't wait that long. What can I do?
(PS – I don't get any pocket money if I don't go.)

I discussed your letter with a Catholic priest and he said he was saddened to think your Dad would bribe you to go to church. Or at least, punish you for not going by withholding your pocket money.

However, I think you are going to have to do what your father wants for a while yet. You know you can probably stop going to church in three years' time. The question is – could you make it more interesting in the meantime, maybe by asking your father to explain the services, or talking to the priest about it? This might also give you a chance to talk about why you have to go to church at all.

Christian in Bermondsey writes:

When they were children, my parents had a lot of brothers and sisters and were very poor, especially my Dad. His family never had as much money as we do.

He wants me to do all the things he never did, but I don't like the things he likes, and this causes a lot of problems.

He forces me to do things. First he made me go to scouts for a year. I didn't like it so, after a big argument, he let me leave. Then it was judo. Exactly the same thing

happened. Now, after another argument, he says I have to
go to judo or play a musical instrument.

Why won't he just leave me alone? Why does he keep
forcing me to do these things?

You know the answer to your own question. You
explained it all in your second paragraph – your
Dad is trying to give *you* the opportunities he never
had as a lad. It's painful for him to learn that you
don't want to do the things he would have given his
eye-teeth to be able to do.

The best way to bear with it is to keep on
suggesting the things you *would* like to do. If you
don't want to throw other boys around on a rubber
mat (judo), would you like to go skating, or water-
skiing, or ride horses? If he wants you to play an
instrument, have you thought of playing something
really fun like the drums? Talk to him like a
grown-up – ask him more questions about his
childhood to help him work through his bad
feelings. You could do him a lot of good! And
yourself.

Mark in Walsall feels stuck:

I have a problem with my brother because he is always
rowing with my mother. He treats her like a lump of dirt
and she gets very hurt. My mother will not tell my father
because she is afraid that he will throw him out of the
house. I think that it is up to me to talk to him. I have talked
to him a few times but he doesn't listen to me. Can you
give me some advice on what I should say to him? My
brother is 17.

I am not sure whether you think you should talk to
your brother about his behaviour, or to your Dad,
but I don't think either conversation would get you

very far. Your brother would simply snarl at you to mind your own business and your Dad might start a big row for which your mother would then blame you. You are not responsible for this problem, so leave it to those who have to face it.

You could ask your Mum why she puts up with it. You could say how bad it makes you feel living in such a miserable house. But beyond that you cannot go. Let things take their course while you get on with your life. In the end your brother will calm down or go too far in which case your Mum *will* have to sort him out.

Hayley from Bideford, now 18, has a happier tale to tell:

I'd like to give people with family problems a sense of hope. When I was 8, my Dad remarried after three years without anyone. I decided I wasn't going to like my step-Mum. After all, we'd managed to get along on our own and didn't need anyone else now, did we?

It wasn't until I eventually left home that I realised how lucky I was to have such a caring step-Mum and Dad, since they gave me so much help and support.

I now see that when she married my Dad, Mum (I soon called her that) had the task of taking on a ready-made family and it must have been hell for her.

If you're prepared to make room for someone else in your heart as well as in your home, instead of pushing them away, it can work.

Finally, let's end this chapter with a letter about a universal problem. The writer is Judy from Halesowen:

Dear Agony Mister,
I admit it, it's true! My bedroom is a really bad tip – BUT I LIKE IT LIKE THAT.

We all get on quite well at home except for this one thing. My Mum is always going on and on and on and on about my room. I think it is *my* room. She shouldn't go in it and I should be allowed to have it any way I want. But when I don't tidy it, after a few weeks she puts everything that's on the floor in a big black rubbish bag and plonks it in the middle of my bed. She says I can't do my homework in the middle of such a mess.

I think she should stay out of my room. What do you think? I know you will agree with me so please tell my Mum to stay out of JUDY'S ROOM! Thanks.

First, a confession. I myself am not the world's tidiest human being and my father once said I would have to leave home if I didn't start hanging up the towels in the bathroom. Family life always has the potential to become very silly although I'm glad I began to see that in the long run it wasn't worth giving a few towels such a hard time!

This is what I think about your problem. Both you and your Mum want something. You both want to be the ruler of your room. She wants to make sure there is no mould growing on the clothes' mountain. You could do a deal. Why not say, 'If you promise to stay out of my room unless I invite you in, I'll promise to clear it up every weekend, make the bed and empty the wastepaper basket. Will you try this and see if it works?' She might take you on.

You would also find that if your room was *never* cleared up, it would become unusable and however 'fragrant' you try to be, the premises would eventually pong. Negotiate – you have nothing to lose and everything to win – unless you are too fond of that interesting game called 'Outwitting Mum'. If so, the fights will continue . . .

CHAPTER 3

FEARS AND PHOBIAS

Fears are sometimes worrying but always exciting.
Think of ghost trains, the Chamber of Horrors and
Dracula films. We often choose to get frightened
because it is so thrilling. But we also get ambushed
by fear sometimes. In fact, our bodies have a whole
'fear system' hooked up to our minds, waiting to
scare the pants off us. Strangely enough, it's there
to protect us *from* the unexpected *by* frightening us!
When there's danger, real or imagined, we *need* to
become instantly prepared so that we can fight or
run away. When creepy things happen, your body
instantly goes into action:

○ your heart pounds
○ your stomach tightens and you even get a kind of
  indigestion feeling
○ blood moves away from your tummy towards
  your arms and legs so you can use your strength
  to run or defend yourself; this can make you feel
  quite sick
○ you sweat, especially on the palms of your hands
○ your mouth goes dry and you may find it hard to
  swallow
○ you get goose bumps
○ the hair along your neck or scalp may stand on
  end
○ you can feel dizzy.

All this is supposed to happen when you are
startled. But fears also happen for particular

reasons, even if those reasons don't seem very clear at first. They need understanding, *not* dismissing. If people don't accept that your fears are important, you feel a heck of a lot worse.

If something unpleasant has happened before and seems about to happen again, you are almost bound to feel afraid. If some boys beat you up in the street on your way home from school once, you'd naturally feel anxious about walking down that street in the future. We are always worried about unpleasant memories coming back to life or by anything that *resembles* a past terror. For example, if you were once frightened by a fat snake you might get frightened by a garden hose pipe lying in the grass that for just one moment *looked* like a snake. You might perhaps be afraid of the dark because you once felt miserable in the dark as a baby and cried when no one came.

So, what are some of the common fears you can have? Let's start with Diane from Ealing:

I am 9 years old and I have an awful fear of fire. I keep on having bad dreams and nightmares about it. Worse, a few weeks ago, we went to a friend's house for dinner. They kept a candle lit and the younger daughter burnt a bracelet over it, and burnt a hole in the tablecloth. When I try to talk to my Mum about it she just says, 'It won't happen, don't worry.' But I think that *however* slight the chance — THE CHANCE IS THERE! Am I wrong?

Cathy in Manchester is afraid of:

. . . going upstairs. My Mum said it's something I will grow out of as I get older but my brain does not agree with that. I am always asking Mum if she will please come up with me. Will you help me with this?

Vanessa from Gloucestershire says:

When I go to bed I shut all my curtains and open my door wide and have the lights on outside my room. But I still think that someone is going to come into my room and kill me or hurt me. I get really scared.

Becca in Dumfries is also bothered by bedtime:

I always think there is someone under my bed or in my wardrobe or behind my door. Even going into the bathroom, I always think there is someone behind the shower curtain.

Sarah in Godalming is another:

I am nearly 13 and have a problem that I think a lot of children have. My problem is that when I go to bed I think there is someone in my room although there is not. When I try and sleep, I hear a person breathing as well – there is no one, of course. But I get so frightened that any little bang or creak makes me jump. Sometimes when my Mum and Dad have gone to bed, I am still awake and cannot get to sleep till nearly 2 am. My problem comes and goes. Sometimes it is very bad. Other times it is not so bad. I think to myself, 'There couldn't be anyone there. I have a dog who would hear someone come in.' But that does not make me feel better. I have told my Dad but he says, 'You've got an imaginative imagination.' I have had this problem for a long time.
(PS – The whole house makes me frightened at night. My room frightens me, but not in daytime.)

Gwynneth in Nottingham hates it:

. . . when I am walking up the library stairs in town. I hate it because the steps have got gaps between them so I have to walk up them really carefully in case my foot gets stuck in the gap. I am 12 this year.

Anthea in Holyhead says:

I have a sort of fear which is like a haunting. I'm always seeing faces of demons that keep saying 'I will get you.' What can I do? You will probably laugh when you get this letter, but it's true.

Blair in Hertford has a different worry:

I am absolutely terrified of PEAS. If someone puts a pea in front of me I either scream or cower away in the corner. I haven't always been scared of peas. When my Mum says I used to eat peas with mashed potato, it makes me cringe. I am 11½.

With Tracey in Bridgnorth it is:

BIRDS. I do not know how long I have had this fear but I think I might have 'inherited' it from my Dad. It is the beaks and wings I am particularly scared of. It does sound a bit babyish but I can't help it.

Lesley from Reigate says:

I can't watch horror films. If I do, after the film I get really scared and can't get to sleep. I go and tell my parents I can't sleep and they just say 'more fool you'. Even my brothers say that, and if I tell my friends they just say 'baby' and 'You're 12 years old and still can't watch a horror film.' As you can imagine, this upsets me very much. Also, all my friends talk about horror films at school so I feel very left out if I don't see them. There's not much more I can say except HELP!

Rosalynn from Chorleywood is terrified of school:

I hate school. In my secondary school, which I started in September, we had exams in the first week which everyone hated and we didn't have time to settle in properly. Every morning before school, I have stomach

ache and I feel sick. I have to get up in the morning at
6.45 am. At 7.50 am I catch the bus. The bus journey
takes about three-quarters of an hour which makes me
even more tensed up as we get nearer school.

Our school is literally a dump but the school for the
second year upwards is in a different building. The ground
nearby is a place where gypsies stay and their dogs have
come into the playground and attacked some of the
children. My worst subject is maths. I didn't mind maths
before we changed teachers. In fact, I got a very good
mark in my exam. Now, though, we have a different
teacher who doesn't explain things and my maths has
gone very much downhill. On a Thursday, we have a
double maths lesson. I feel so sick in these lessons and
feel like bursting into tears. One day, my friend and I tried
to ask the teacher what we were supposed to do and she
went mad. She said 'You weren't listening' and she
refused to tell us how to do it. How do you deal with
problems like these?

Many, including Naomi of Hampstead, suffer from the same problem:

I'm scared stiff to go to school. My Dad doesn't listen to
me when I tell him about this and he always expects me to
do better with my school work than I think I can. I try as
hard as possible to do my best but it never comes up to
the standard which my Dad wants it to. He always shouts
at me if I haven't done well.

Jonathan in Mitcham says:

There is a particular teacher I'm really frightened of. I have
her once a week for music and she worries me to death.
She shouts a lot and we normally have to work in groups,
which doesn't help because I'm shy and nobody will join
up with me.

Camilla in Slough has:

. . . a great fear of having to read from a book or play when I get to school.

I've tried to talk to my English teacher about this but he doesn't seem to understand. He says he will still make me read aloud when my turn comes round.

I used to be very extrovert and used to do assembly in front of the whole school. But I have now gone totally the other way and would prefer to be put in detention rather than have to recite in front of the class. My stomach turns somersaults and I get all sweaty and feel like I'm going to faint. Once, when the teacher told me to read, I even started to cry just to get out of it. I am 14 years old and worry about this terribly.

Finally on school fears, let's hear from Linda in West Yorkshire:

When fears were being discussed on TV last Saturday, you mentioned that they can stem from something that seems totally separate from the actual fear itself.

This reminded me of a school fear I had when I was 8 years old (I am now 30). For some unknown reason, I suddenly refused to go to school. My poor Mum tried everything from gentle persuasion to literally dragging me there and in desperation she also took me to a child specialist.

My grandmother was very ill at the time and died, and it was discovered that I was blaming myself for her illness – I would not leave my mother in case something happened to her too. I was persuaded to talk about any feelings I had and after a week at home to settle down, off I trotted to school as happily as before.

So you can see that my fear of school wasn't directly linked to school at all!

Moving on from school, Mike in Grimsby hates his feelings about dogs:

I am 13 years old and very small for my age. I have been terrified of dogs since I was young. The trouble is that there are seven dogs in my road, from a Jack Russell to an alsatian. I live between the alsatian and a golden labrador. My front door is down the side of the house. When I go out, the golden labrador jumps right up to the fence. I then come back in shaking. If I get past that dog, I have to try and run the gauntlet of the alsatian. After all this I have to go through the same thing when I come back. This fear is very bad because I am being stopped from going out, which I need to do.

We all need to go out, and Cheryl from Aylesbury is someone who has managed it:

When I was little I used to be terrified of dogs. My Mum always had to take me to school, as I couldn't go on my own with dogs about. When we went to my cousin's, 'Charlie' (their retriever) had to be locked in their car before I would enter the house.

But since I was about 10, everything has changed. I am now madly in love with dogs and have a King Charles spaniel and one day hope to breed them. That just goes to show you that fears can go away.

Before we get on to 'phobias', let's take a look at what you can do about the fears already mentioned. I'd say to Diane (who was worried about fires) that her Mum is trying to give her reassurance, but it's come out the wrong way. Get Mum to say to you 'I can see that you're worried about this love' which is much better than 'Fires are rare' or even 'Fires don't happen' because of course we all know that they do. And it tells you that she's listening and accepting your worries. Ask her to listen to you describing some of your dreams and nightmares so you can gradually come to feel that nightmares are really quite ordinary. She may even tell you about some of her own nightmares – because we *all* have them. Your real problem is *not feeling very safe* and *not having your feelings accepted*. As a result, you focus on what may go wrong as though it *must* go wrong and get the hazards of fire out of all proportion.

As for fears about bodies in the wardrobe, under the bed, on the stairs, in the attic, or fears about nasties in the night who are coming to get you, these are all perfectly understandable and have a meaning. All animals, including us, are a bit frightened of the dark and night-time. There are two reasons for this. First, we can't see what is going on around us and therefore we are less in control of our safety. Secondly, we need to fall asleep and that means becoming unconscious. When we're unconscious, we have to trust that we will wake up again and that nothing will attack us while we're alone and helpless. We need to work out how to trust the dark. Every child has to learn to do this and if parents aren't very helpful or patient, it takes a lot of extra work and worry.

It's much more difficult if you've been through any other frightening experiences in your life because you'll almost certainly feel a bit less safe when you have to go to bed. The fear will strike before you know it and you need to realise that it isn't actually about 'someone being in the room'. It's really about you feeling jumpy and insecure generally.

As in so many cases, you have to try and educate your parents to understand your needs. Get them to help you step by step. Say you suffer from these fears and are trying to deal with them. Routine is always comforting. You might like your Mum or Dad to walk you all the way to the top of the stairs one week, then to the top but one step the second week and one step lower each week till you feel safe climbing upstairs by yourself. Above all, get the adults to say 'I can see you're worried about this' rather than 'Don't be silly, there's nothing there!' Show them this page if you want. Then talk to your parents generally about things on your mind, or other worries. It will be a *relief*.

With fears like Gwynneth's (the library steps), tell yourself how often you have already managed to face your problem successfully. Your body is, in fact, more reliable than you think it is, isn't it? Worries about peas, Blair, can be dealt with by realising that you are having a battle of wills with Mum about what you should eat, rather than anything more sinister. Perhaps the best way to prove this, would be to buy a packet of peas from the garden centre, grow some in a pot and get to know them from the ground up.

With horror films (Lesley's problem), the fact has to be faced that they are intended to scare you and you need to be very used to them to feel unaffected. One tip: draw a picture of a camera on a piece of paper next time you look at something too scary and keep reminding yourself that what you see on the telly is not real because it had to be shot by a camera with a crew of men and women who are just doing a job of work. Look at the drawing to keep this thought in your head. If the picture on the screen were *real*, there couldn't be a film of it – especially if it's about a werewolf, because he'd smash the camera and chase the crew!

As for dogs, enlist the help of grown-ups – not to take you to school, but to see whether any neighbouring pets are *able* to get at you or are safely prevented by fences. If they can't get at you, then walk past with your fingers in your ears looking straight ahead. After a while you'll learn that the journey is genuinely safe.

Fears and panics about school are common. I suffered terribly with my maths teacher (who was an awful bully) when I was 6, and actually tried to stay awake all night so that morning would take longer to arrive. The most sensible way to tackle the trouble is to talk to your parents or another teacher, saying that you are falling behind in the subject in question. Being able to get a hearing will make you feel more effective and less depressed. You don't just have to put up with what is dished out. If shyness or self-consciousness make you afraid to go to school, tackle them. Not going to school won't help you feel any more confident. Practise reading aloud at home in front of the mirror. Rehearse the things that you think are going to be difficult and remember that none of us find performing or mixing *easy*.

In answer to Linda's letter, yes, in many cases the problem of not wanting to go somewhere is really about what you are afraid to *leave behind*, in your example a Mum who might die – until it was explained to you that this was not likely, it just *felt* likely. And this is a very normal reaction when someone close is taken from us. If your Mum had not been sensible and realised that your problem needed special help, maybe you would have developed full-blown school phobia with panic and fainting attacks.

'Phobias' are big fears. Your body and mind go

into a sort of 'red alert' when something really frightens you or you imagine that something is very dangerous. You begin to panic. You may be so terrified that you cannot run away. You feel as if you are rooted to the spot. When you do regain control of your legs, you run like mad. Obviously, running away makes you feel better but only because you have *avoided* the problem. To keep calm in future, you have to go on avoiding *all* similar situations. So if you felt panic on a train (and got off) or in a lift (and got out) or when faced by a spider (and left the bathroom), you are now afraid your fear will return if you ever get back on to a train, into a lift or try to take a spider out of the bath. You have taught yourself to be 'phobic'. Everyone is mildly phobic about something. I can't stand flying in aeroplanes, although I do it when I have to. But when your phobia spoils your life, it needs tackling.

Doreen from Surrey has a phobic response to injections:

I was not too bothered about them when I was younger but have recently become frightened of them after a blood test. Now, when I go to the doctor or dentist or visit someone in hospital, I get dizzy and faint. The mere mention of an injection or seeing it on TV turns me into a nervous wreck.

Should I go and give blood in order to face my phobia? I feel I cannot. Why is it that anything to do with injections makes me feel sick and dizzy?

The next letter is from a grown-up, but her fears are just as strong:

Dear *Growing Pains*,
I get so panic-stricken when a storm is overhead that I try

to hide behind a door where I cannot see it. I dread storms, especially in the summer when they are most frequent, and as I live alone it makes the problem twice as nerve-racking for me. During the night if there is a storm I cannot bear to stay in bed. I often have to go downstairs and prepare a hot drink to relax my nerves, as I just go to pieces.

Can you give me any helpful advice? I know your programme is for teenagers but I feel desperate for some assistance.

Hassan from Leicester is 15 but his feelings (and words) are almost identical:

I've been terrified of thunderstorms for some years now and, as much as I want to, I just can't get over them.

I get absolutely petrified if it gets dark during the day and we have very heavy rain. I dread the summer coming because it always ends in a thunderstorm and when we have one I lie face down on my bed so I don't see the flashes of lightning. It may seem childish but it screws me up. I've been out in storms with my Dad but even this does not help me to face up to the situation.

I want to get over this phobia, since I will soon be 16 and will eventually have to get a job and perhaps marry and have children of my own, and I would not be much of a parent if I ran away from the weather, would I?

I have watched programmes on why we have thunderstorms and read books on them, but whenever we have one I am practically in tears. My parents, family, teachers and friends have tried to get me over this phobia but although I want to I just can't bring myself to accept it. Whenever we have a storm I say to myself, 'Pull yourself together – everyone else just carries on as normal, and so can you!' But it continues to ruin my life.

Sally in Devon is also phobic:

Last week, your show was about fears and phobias. Well, I have a very strange phobia. I am absolutely petrified of people being sick. Even knowing that someone is being sick really does frighten me. I started to realise that I had this fear when I saw a drunken man being sick and that night I was so scared I couldn't sleep, and now whenever anyone is sick on telly or talks about it I have to run away. I think about things that have nothing to do with the man being sick. Can you help? Please could you find someone with the same fear? Or tell me if it's a normal fear?

Magnus in London says:

I start to panic if anyone offers me food in the evening. I've been told that if you eat anything after 7 pm it turns straight into fat. Well, I go swimming around 7 to 9 each evening so when I get home I am pretty hungry. If I ate would the food turn into fat or not?
(PS – I am mad on digestive biscuits.)

Katie from Belfast says:

I am nearly 15 and suffer from more phobias than one. I am terrified of spiders, pigeons and worms. I cannot bear being in a closed room. I must have the door open at all times. I also hate being in open spaces on my own. I had a fainting attack once when I was in church because I looked up and the roof was so high. I am sick when I look over a low balcony.

These phobias are common but the main one I want to overcome is sleep. I hate sleeping. I scare myself thinking that I won't wake up or that the bomb is going to drop. Before I go to bed I write a letter to my family and boyfriend saying that if I don't wake up, they should give my body to medical research.

Sometimes I stay on the telephone to my friends for

hours. When I start to get tired, I write song lyrics or play music very loud so it helps me to keep awake. I've been offered wake-up pills by friends who know of my problems. I've tried this once and it helped a bit but there must be another way to overcome this illness? I once wanted to sleep because I had been awake for 24 hours. I slept for 3 hours but woke up sweating and shaking. I hope you can help me.

Tracy from Biggin Hill says:

If I see a spider I scream. I HATE THEM. I don't know why I hate them because they are harmless but I could never have a tarantula or one of those great big hairy-legged things crawling up my arm.

One of my Mum's friends went to a hypnotist because she was terrified of spiders. The hypnotist started by putting little money spiders into her hand and, gradually, got on to bigger and bigger ones until she had a tarantula in her hand. I could not ever hold one, even if I was paid £10,000!

I can't even look at pictures of them because I get nightmares, and if I see a tiny spider crawling up the wall, I have bad dreams about it. I also hate earwigs and beetles. I used to be OK with beetles until a boy put one down my neck. I was absolutely terrified! He said it was dead but . . . it wasn't. I could feel it crawling down my back. Every time I see a beetle now it reminds me of that.

Really, I hate all insects although I would never kill any. I am now 14.

And, last in this section, Mrs James from Airdrie writes about her son:

My son has a phobia. When he goes out he keeps checking that everything is in order. When he eventually gets out, he may be halfway up the road and he comes back to check that the gate is closed or that the dog is in.

He has on occasions telephoned to ask if everything is as it should be.

I'd be grateful for some advice on your programme as I don't know how to handle this phobia. Thanks.

Firstly, Mrs James, your son has *not* got a phobia. He is suffering from what is called obsessive anxiety or anxiety 'neurosis'. This only means he's dead worried about making mistakes, letting you down or causing a disaster. It's quite a common difficulty especially if someone has been brought up fairly strictly and constantly warned to 'get it right'. I don't know if this has happened to Billy. The anxiety often affects people when they have to cope entirely on their own. Billy is taking too much responsibility for his life and my advice to you would be to 'baby' him a bit more, relax the rules and offer him more treats and rewards. You might even let him know about some of the times in your life when you've made mistakes, so he feels he has 'permission' to do the same. I believe we all need to feel we have a 'margin for error'. Don't you?

It's also hard to say that the very common fear of spiders (mentioned by Katie) is a phobia pure and simple. Most people who are terrified of these good and useful creatures have never been bitten or frightened by them *before* they hate them. It's as if they are *born* with an instinctive horror of *spideriness*. They don't like the *sight* of creepy-crawly movements and even though British spiders are so harmless you could take them to bed with you (ugh!, did you say?), the fact remains that people hate the *idea* of a spider's jaws piercing a fly and sucking it dry. Spiders also live in the *dark* and spin *webs* which *trap* unsuspecting creatures (even if flies are usually pretty dirty and capable of spreading diseases wherever we leave food).

So the problem with spiders is what they suggest in our minds – feelings of insecurity, being trapped, being crept up on or ambushed, feelings of being afraid of fear itself, since it's hard to tell the difference between a spider crawling up your neck and your hair standing on end all by itself. The best thing Tracy can do is to share her fears instead of treating them as closed books of horror she cannot talk about. Describe these nightmares. Talk about times when she's felt alone and afraid as a child. Write letters to herself about these terrible creatures, so she can get more familiar and comfortable with her terrors. Then maybe draw the odd spider picture . . .

Katie's letter shows her to be phobic in general and I suspect some pretty terrible things *have* happened in her life. She writes as if she's all alone, although she must have someone looking after her, and this terror of falling asleep suggests that there is a real fear of being attacked. It's as if she's saying she needs to be on permanent guard duty. I think Katie ought to ask at school for an appointment with a child psychologist and look into things generally, not just into phobias.

We can probably stop Magnus (who is worried about his weight) becoming phobic at all. No, it's not true that everything you eat after 7 pm turns to fat – especially if you are burning up lots of calories by swimming for a couples of hours beforehand. Food doesn't turn straight into fat at any time of the day, although the sugar in biscuits won't give you any nourishment. Tip: there are fewer calories in a wholemeal bread and tomato sandwich with a little butter on it than just *two* digestive biscuits (and I suggest you also read the chapter called Fats and thins, talls and smalls).

When it comes to classic phobias like those of Doreen and Hassan about injections and thunderstorms, the treatment is relatively simple:

● Stop saying you're 'silly'. Part of the problem is not having enough respect for your fears and worries and only looking at them through the eyes of parents and others. Anybody can become phobic under the right conditions and your feeling of *fear* is real – just like all feelings are 'real', aren't they? Nobody enjoys having needles stuck in them or being deafened by thunderbolts. You have reacted to your own natural sense of *shock* more strongly because you did not feel entitled to run to someone for comfort or have not been able to cry when the needle slipped and hurt quite a lot. If it's thunder that bothers you, there is also this fact: electrical storms do affect some people more strongly than others, making them more anxious and depressed. It is not that you are going mad or that you are going to be killed.

● Accept that avoidance cannot work – we all need injections sometimes and there is no place to hide from thunder.

● Learn a relaxation technique so that when you next find the symptoms of panic arising, you can slow your breathing and *reverse* the changes that acute anxiety produces in your body. It is impossible to be calm and in a panic at the same time. When you eventually achieve a state of control while sitting in the dentist's chair or while a storm is gathering, you will feel immensely *pleased* and *happy*.

● Consciously think about what scares you most.

Start with talking. Make drawings of syringes and bad weather. Buy a nurse's kit with a toy syringe. Talk to others about feeling ill and what might happen to you. Did somebody dear to you once die in hospital for instance, or during a storm? This might be part of the problem. Then, when you're feeling more comfortable, and you're sure the relaxation exercise has been mastered, boldly make a dental appointment, start watching films you know have storm scenes in them, or play recordings you can get of bad weather 'sound effects'.

In answer to Sally, phobias about people being sick are quite common and can be dealt with in the same way as other phobias.

Relaxation exercises can be learned from cassettes sold by post. For further details, send a stamped addressed envelope to Relaxation for Living, 29 Burwood Park Road, Walton-On-Thames, KT12 5LH. The Phobics' Society is at 4 Cheltenham Road, Chorlton-Cum-Hardy, Manchester M21 1QN. They have loads of self-help leaflets on combatting fears and panics.

CHAPTER 4

(ODY) (DOUR)

One of the reasons why people think children are sweet is that they usually don't smell as much as grown-ups. Adults have what are called 'apocrine' sweat glands which produce masses of stinky sweat, particularly under their arms. Children don't. But as children *become* adults, in the teenage years, they develop these glands and can begin to worry about their new and noticeable grown-up pong.

This pong is naturally made worse if it's old pong. Fresh sweat isn't too bad – some people like the aroma. But stale sweat actually starts to rot and most things that rot also stink. This is just one reason why it's a good idea to wash your *whole* body every day, to change your underclothes *every day* and to get your other clothes dry-cleaned as often as possible. (We British have a bad reputation for hygiene and one of the dead giveaways is stale sweat.)

Mr Anonymous from Worcestershire has a perspiration problem:

I am writing to you because I have a problem which I cannot control. The problem I am referring to is body odour (BO). I wash all over every morning with soap and water, then I dry myself and put some deodorant on. By the middle of the day, my armpits are sweaty, smelly and wet, and when I get up from sitting on a plastic seat there is a great wet patch where my bottom has been. What should I do?

Even worse, when I do sport all my friends are hardly sweating while I am pouring with the stuff. It's totally embarrassing. Please can you help me? I am 14 years old and need your urgent help.

First, you should understand that we sweat when we need to lose heat. It's the body's way of putting liquid on the surface of the skin so that heat is lost more rapidly as the sweat dries in the air. We get rid of up to 2 litres of water a day from our bodies, much of it by sweating. You will obviously sweat more if you are overweight (because fat makes you hot) and if you drink a lot – so those are two things you *could* control. Secondly, as I say, washing won't get rid of smells unless you also keep your clothes clean and change your underwear daily. Thirdly, make sure you buy cotton not synthetic materials for underwear and shirts. If you have to sit on a plastic chair, put some paper or a cushion on it first. Fourth, as your body is going through its growing-up phase, you may find that it takes a while for the system to settle down and not *over-produce* sweat. Anxiety also makes you perspire more. Fifth, don't eat too much spicy food – the smell comes out in your sweat. Sixth, if you are really worried see your GP, since there are some conditions where sweating *is* excessive for medical reasons.

When Mr Anonymous's letter was read out on TV, a number of people wrote in with helpful comments or suggestions.

There was Mrs Anonymous in Teddington:

Dear All,
I'm a Mum who happened to be looking in on Saturday and heard the *Growing Pains* item where a teenager was

worried about BO.

As a teenager and indeed up to a few years ago, I went through much embarrassment and misery with just the same problem. I used to dread taking off my cardigan at school because of those awful wet marks under the arms on my dress. I'll never forget how wretched it was and I felt really sorry for Mr Anonymous whose letter sounded just as desperate as I felt. However, I have discovered an antiperspirant which really does act effectively and has changed my life. (I know that sounds extravagant but it has helped tremendously.) If you have his address, *please* tell the teenager about Odaban, which should be available from chemists as a roll-on. It is manufactured at Bracey's Pharmacy, 6 West Way, Liverpool L31 0DQ.

And Mrs Chambers in Leeds adds:

I had this problem for 18 years and the wetness was horrendous! In desperation, I saw my doctor and enquired about cosmetic surgery (I believe you can have some of the sweat glands surgically removed) and he in turn contacted a specialist who put me on to a roll-on type deodorant called Driclor which is available on prescription. The effect after a couple of weeks of nightly use was amazing. The wetness vanished and now, 2 years later, I seldom need to apply it. It boosted my self-confidence no end.

So, possibly, *worrying* about sweating too much was part of the *cause* of Mrs Chambers' problem. Other types of BO also abound, as Cora in Norwich makes clear:

Dear *Growing Pains*,

I have a problem – my feet always smell and I change my socks every day. Everybody says 'Poo, what's that smell?' and I get very embarrassed. What *shall* I do?

Well, Cora, if it's not your feet (because you wash them) and it's not your socks (because you change them), it's got to be your shoes, hasn't it? There are deodorant pads you can put in the bottoms of your shoes to deal with this difficulty but some shoes are just too far gone – impregnated with old stale smells. Have a sniff and see if I'm right. (And try to avoid wearing shoes made of synthetics.)

Bernard in Rotherham is bothered by:

Bad Breath. It is a very shameful problem and I find that I'm unable to speak to anyone face to face anymore, as I am told by friends that I have bad breath. I used to be very free and easy talking with girls but now when I go out they think I'm shy even though I am not.

This problem is worrying me a lot. I haven't told my mother about it and daren't even ask the dentist for help. What can I do?

First, try and work out whether this really is part of your shyness (even though you deny it). Look at the chapter in this book on that subject. Are you really saying you think your breath *always* smells, or that you just got embarrassed on one occasion when there was a good reason why your breath should have been noticeably stale or spicy? You were obviously very embarrassed when your friends told you about it.

If the problem is more persistent, this is the way to think about it, in five main areas:

● Teeth. You haven't talked to the dentist but it's a good idea to do so. If there are food particles between your teeth they will decay and start to smell. Use dental floss, a special string you can buy from the chemist to remove any muck that's stuck in your mouth. Don't try to saw your teeth out – pull the string between a couple of teeth in turn and gently lift the debris away. Make sure you clear the 'underhangs' near the gums where disease can start. Ask the dentist or the dental hygienist to scrape away any old dental plaque which can also contribute to the problem. Clean your teeth *and gums* (gum disease smells too) every day. An anti-fungal mouthwash, such as Oraldene, is also a great help.

- Food. What's in your stomach doesn't make a smell in the outside world (unless you belch or vomit) because your stomach is protected by the gullet. But food can make your breath smell, via your lungs. The 'smell molecules' in garlic, onions, curries, beer, wine, etc. get carried through your bloodstream from your stomach into your lungs where you breathe them over people. (These smells can also contribute to BO through your sweat glands.) It would clearly be a good idea to experiment with a diet that did not include strong-smelling foods.

- Infection. Do you have any mouth ulcers or are there any places on your tongue or in your mouth which are sore? These can give rise to odours and you should see your doctor if they persist for more than a couple of weeks.

- Smoking. It makes *all* of you smell and the remedy is in your own fingers – don't smoke.

- Some feverish illnesses also cause bad breath, but this is not your problem and I only mention it for completeness.

CHAPTER 5

PERIODS

Having a first period should be a moment of pride for a girl and an event that builds up personal confidence. Alas, it is not always so. In fact I decided to write this book after receiving the following sad letter from Ruth in Scotland:

Dear *Growing Pains*,
I have a pain in my tummy and my Mum thinks that I am starting my periods. I don't know anything about them – like when they start – and my Mum won't tell me about it. I am worried. Please could you tell me what I should do? I am nearly 10.

Gillian, aged 12, says:

I think you should talk about periods because girls at the age of 10 or 11 might be afraid of them even if their mothers have talked about them. I have not had my periods yet.

Tara from Oxford writes:

I have had pains around my chest lately. I've had them ever since February. In July, my bust was 30A and on 1 September I was size 32AA. Later in the month I got a bra and I was size 32A. It is still very painful but it helped a bit. It stopped them from hurting when I ran. It hurts most around my hips and my vagina and I have quite a lot of discharge, mostly at nights. Now I know that it is not going to be easy being a woman and I am afraid of starting my periods. I am only 10.

Miss X in Anglesey says:

My problem is that I have started my period and I am 11 years old and nobody else in our class has started. After we have had hockey we *have* to go in the shower. I worry about it a lot because being the only one who has developed is very hard for me. I could never tell my teacher because I am too shy. I hope you can help me to deal with this and tell me what I should do.

Maria in Bury St Edmunds writes:

I have a problem. I am 12 years old and I have started my period and I am often in a lot of pain. I also get very moody and my friends keep taking the mickey out of me so I snap at them. If I don't watch out I won't have any friends left. Also, my breasts are developing and it hurts.

The girls from Form 3b in a convent in Scotland write:

Please tell us all about GROWING PAINS. We think this is a very important subject. And we need help.

Mandy in Derby writes:

I feel very embarrassed writing in about this kind of problem but I really want to know about it. Sometimes, when I am in my bed, I get sharp pains in my vagina. It hurts a lot and I cannot sleep. When it happens, it sometimes goes on for at least half an hour. It also happens at school. I am very worried about it. I hope it is not infected. Please mention this because I have to know as soon as possible. I just hope it is not infected because I have heard a lot about vaginal infections. I am 11 but I have not started my periods yet.

And Megan in Caernarfon says:

I'm writing this to you because I know you can sympathise

with my problem. I am 14½ years old and have not yet started my periods. This did not bother me too much until last week. I fell out with my best friend and she went around telling everyone about my problem – including my boyfriend. Although he is very understanding, I cannot say the same for the other people she has told. They have started calling me things like 'baby' and I get very upset. I sometimes even cry myself to sleep at night. Please help.

This group of letters (a few of many) are about the *original* growing pain – having a first period. It's tragic if you are *not* prepared for what is to happen by your mother or others in your family. It can be scary if what are perfectly normal symptoms, sometimes of discomfort, are not properly explained. I think we have to accept that some parents cannot talk about these matters. They feel embarrassed. Perhaps their parents did not talk to them when they were young. But having growing-up pains is *nothing* to be ashamed about.

If you can't talk to your Mum, then try speaking to someone you feel comfortable with, who does have periods – such as an older sister, aunt or teacher – and put direct questions. Yes, Tara, all your symptoms show that you are about to start your periods. The discharge is the most convincing sign. You will probably get an aching back and some more tummy pains before you really begin, but these are normal – and rest and a hot-water bottle might help. Make sure you are equipped by your Mum to deal with the first flow.

British girls generally start their periods at any age between 10 and 16, with most beginning between 11 and 14, and this variation is due to factors like when your Mum started hers, how big you are and how your individual body works (faster or slower). Periods are generally irregular at first. If people tease you (Megan) because you haven't started yet, you could always say 'the sooner you start the sooner you stop', which is true. The best answer is to say that since you're not God, you can't decide these things anyway.

The next best answer is to get as much information on the subject as possible and I would recommend a book called *Have You Started Yet?* by Ruth Thomson (published by Piccolo at £1.50). If you become an expert on yourself you will always be able to show your critics that they are less well-informed than they think, and that nearly always shuts people up. By the way, Ruth Thomson says you can deal with cramps and stabbing pains by trying out any of the following:

○ not moving about too much – sitting up straight and maybe taking a paracetamol
○ exercising – it's tough at first, but feels good afterwards
○ walking, drinking lots of water and getting an early night or two
○ making sure you eat well to keep up your energy
○ taking extra Vitamin C
○ massaging your stomach and the bottom of your spine with your knuckles really hard
○ lying on your back with your knees up
○ relaxing and breathing deeply
○ taking a long bath and going to bed with a cup of tea – sometimes, lying on your tummy will help.

A word of caution. Although it is unlikely that you will have a pelvic infection, you should always discuss strong and persistent pains with your GP. Similarly, if you have very bad mood swings before your period, your doctor is there to help.

CHAPTER 6

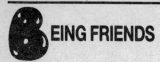 **EING FRIENDS**

I assure you it gets better later on in life (well a bit), but teenage and pre- teenage friendships seem jolly difficult to make and keep. People seem to behave in the most heartless way, dropping you at a moment's notice – then telling all your mutual friends it's because you've got a great big blue mark on your bottom and a toad living in your hair! Your letters divide into two groups – those worried about friends or best friends of the *same* sex, and those about the girlfriend or boyfriend blues. We'll start on the first set with Alison who comes from West Bromwich:

I'm writing to tell you about my terrible problem with school. I am in the first year at a private school. When I started off, I didn't know many people. After the first month, I was beginning to make friends. Then one or two people said a few nasty things about me. They were not true. Now I don't have any friends. I try to talk to the children and be friendly but it is no good. They think I am common. But they are the ones who are stuck-up.

I have never really liked school but I was pretty popular at my last school. When I am at school I feel ill and nearly fall asleep in class. My work is bad and untidy because I am so depressed. I really try to smile. I have skived off or pretended I was sick a few times. Out of school, life is really brilliant and I have loads of friends. I am leaving this place soon. I would like to go to drama school. How do I cope with this awful place? I am 12.

Tamsin in Suffolk writes:

The problem I have is friends. It all started when my best friend made friends with a bully. The bully, who is called Marjorie, let my friend Liz on to her table at school and I moved with her. Ben, who sat at the table, did not like me because of my curly hair. He then started calling me 'ambush' and 'square ambush'. Then one day I came home with bruises up my legs from when I could not stop myself kicking him. I moved off the table but now I have lost a best friend. Please help.

And Caroline from Wisbech says:

Dear Phillip,
I am 13 and have sat on my own at school for over a year. When I first came to the senior school with all the other new children, I sat at a table with friends. One morning I came in and Vera, who sat at the same table as me, told me to go away and sit somewhere else. I asked her the next day if I could come back and she said 'No'. And from then on, nobody has seemed to want to sit with me.

There's only one boy in my class who isn't like 'them', and he's nice to me. Every time we go into different classes for another lesson, everybody moves away from me. I've been kicked and punched a lot by people who aren't in my class. I sometimes think it's my clothes (because they're not as fashionable as theirs) or it's my funny hairstyle. It makes me feel very depressed a lot of the time and sometimes I feel suicidal.

Although I have no friends in my class, I have two other friends in different classes who I hang about with at lunchtimes. I know it might not sound much of a problem but it really gets me down. My form-teacher has spoken to the children before, to ask them if they can be friendly, but it only lasts for about two days. At home, I have nothing to do except listen to the radio. What can I do?

And there's Mark in Scunthorpe:

My problem is that I miss my brother who is my best friend and away at university. Could you tell me how to overcome this please?

Catherine in Cambridge feels:

. . . more mature than the other girls in my class. In the playground all the girls play games like Pink Windmill. I am an only child aged 10 and get very lonely in my road where all the girls are aged over 12 or are around 4, 5 or 6. Please, please, please could you help me?

Maxine in Carlisle says:

When I first went to senior school I didn't have a friend to go around with. Then a new girl came and we became best friends until halfway through the second year when she (I will call her Sim) started ignoring me and going round with someone else. They are now best friends. I have tried making friends with someone else but they have got other friends who I don't know and they boss me around a lot and don't speak to me much. Then I see Sim enjoying herself with her new friend and I feel depressed.

Ellie in Avon also knows this terrible feeling:

I have this problem – it's my friend. At the end of last year, we got on very well but then she started to go off with my other friend and she has been awful to me. She tells me what she thinks of everything and it's getting to the stage where it's really hurting me. Everything has got to be her way. Then, if you do something she doesn't like, she'll go off and talk about you. At night, when we go out, as soon as her new friend comes on the scene, that's me out of the way and I might as well not be there. I end up crying. It doesn't sound much to be crying over but if you knew her you'd understand. Sometimes we do sit and talk things over between ourselves and she says she won't do it again. My parents say it's my age. My sister doesn't listen – I suppose the answer is that everybody talks about everyone and everybody uses everybody. I would just like a simple solution.

Another sad story comes from Teri in Burnley:

I am 14 years of age and am in my third year at secondary school. I have a problem with my two friends, Diana and Teresa. I started hanging around with them in my second year and I was dead glad because we were all friends together. Diana was sort of the leader (all mouth and orders), Teresa was dead soft and did anything she was told, and then there was me. I wasn't that stupid but I got carried away. Anyway, the other day we had a little argument that turned into a big one and now we're not speaking to each other. Teresa and Diana are together and I'm left out. Diana has got Teresa wrapped round her little finger. It's just that Diana doesn't seem to understand that I've got feelings too. I really want to leave them and forget about them because I know they're not worth it, but I just can't because I haven't got any other friends, apart from Thelma who is really nice. She keeps telling me to leave them and hang round with her but I don't know if I really want to. I'm so confused. I know this letter sounds stupid but I can't help thinking about it and sometimes it makes me cry. How can I get them to be friends with me again?

Let's try and look at what friendship is all about. First, it's a way of joining a special group or partnership. Us against them. We're special. Second, it's about looking after each other's needs – 'I'll scratch your back if you'll scratch mine' sort of thing. Third, it makes you have a lot of feelings that can hurt you, feelings of what's called *vulnera-*

bility. If you like someone enough to be their best friend you can be made to feel awful if the friendship is lost. Above all, it's very easy to get *jealous*. Fourth, it's hard to know whether these bad feelings are just reactions to what's happening inside the friendship, or whether it's made worse by similar feelings you may have had previously in the family about parents or brothers and sisters. What I mean is this: sometimes, you are not just jealous about your friend betraying you but desperate because you feel this has been the story of your life. Parents and family have always let you down. Now a friend has gone and done the selfsame thing. As a result, you over-react with the friend, who may not understand why you think they've been *so* awful. Fifth, it's inevitable anyway that friendships come and go. People enter and leave our lives and we can't help it. This doesn't mean we'll never have any more friends. It just sometimes *feels that way*.

So try not to see everything in *black and white*; as *all or nothing*; as *hit or miss*. If someone insults you, or tells you to go away, or lets you down, it does *not* mean they hate you, or never want to see you again or can't be a real support on another occasion. We are not perfect, nor meant to be. I'm certainly not. Are you? Nor are they. Roll with the punches, as they say. Try to see that things will go wrong from time to time but that this is not the end of the world. You cannot force people to be friendly with you. But you can get them more interested in being with you if you offer them something – if you are the person with the ideas about what to play next and how to play it. If you are the one who doesn't boast but really does know how steam engines work or who's in which pop group – and can talk sensibly about these things. If people are flatly rejecting, don't keep asking for more, of course, but seek out the ones who *have* got time for you. Find out about *them* and their interests, hobbies, private lives.

So, Alison, I realise it's hard to break the ice at a new school. Yet you know you are pretty good at making friends. You did it at your old school. You have friends outside your present school. All you have to do is accept that you're now making a new start, from the bottom again. Who's the least unfriendly person in your present class? Ask that person over to your home. Go on, you've nothing to lose. Don't decide in advance that they're too snooty for you. That's just you protecting your pride.

For the rest, who feel they have lost a friend and cannot get past that point, try to accept that we sometimes have to put up with this and it has advantages. There were probably things about the person in question you did *not* like so much. Well, now you don't have to put up with the bad bits, even if you've lost the good parts. It's said that as one door closes, another opens – every ending is also a beginning. And if you don't have a current best friend, it increases your chances of getting one because the opportunity now exists. You're not already 'spoken for'. Especially, Catherine, if you learn how to negotiate. Why *not* play Pink Windmill, even though you hate it, thereby making people enjoy your company, and then suggest a game you *would* like to take part in? Somebody in the group might think you are the sort they'd like for a best friend!

Obviously, a lot of this also applies to friendships with the opposite sex as well, but there are some special difficulties here, such as the situation Michael in Greenwich has experienced:

Dear Phillip,

You may have seen the BBC *News* one day in which a man and his daughter who survived the Zeebrugge ferry disaster were featured. They were returning to the scene to thank the doctors and rescuers who saved their lives. They also visited the actual spot in the sea where the ferry went over. The girl was rescued by helicopter, taken to hospital but pronounced dead on arrival because her heart was not beating – then she woke up and is now fit and well.

I really admired her courage in going back to the scene of the disaster. In fact, I admired her so much that after a few hours I found that I had fallen in love with her. At the moment, I cannot get her off my mind which is a bit annoying because I am just about to take my O-levels. What can I do? I am desperate to get in touch with her after my exams. How do I go about doing this? I love her so much.

Penny in Sunderland complains:

I am writing to tell you about my problem with boys. I am 12 years of age and boys don't bat an eyelid at me. I must tell you that I wear glasses and I am a bit fat but that doesn't make me unable to go out with boys. When I go shopping with my friends they all have boys to cuddle up to and I have no one. Please will you help me? The boys just don't seem to fancy me anymore.

Anne in Southampton, also 12, does have a fella:

I have one very special problem – my friend. He is very handsome. I love him. The thing is that I need some expert advice because he always calls me 'sexy' and 'darling', and he says he loves me but the way he says it, I don't know if he really loves me and I am just desperate to know. I am 12.

Jennie in Pulborough writes:

I am 14½ years old and I have been going out with a 15-year-old boy for two months and a week, when suddenly he falls out with me – no argument or anything – he just says I act childish. I'm not shy and I like being with people. I must admit I act a little daft sometimes but only if people around me look gloomy, so what can I do?

And Cheryl in Darlaston says:

I am writing to tell you about this boy that I know at school. I've really liked him since the first year and at last he asked me out and I said 'Yes' of course. But after about three days he finished with me because he said that I never talked to him, and I am really upset. Please help me.

Nigel in Wythenshawe writes:

I met a girl at a friend's party and liked her at once. We lived (or live) on different sides of Manchester so I didn't see her again until a month later at another party. The next week, I asked her out and she said 'Yes'. We went out a few times and got on very well until one night at a disco when she chucked me, and went out with another boy.

Although she was my first girlfriend and although I was very, very upset I said to myself 'Never mind, you'll get over her.' But I never have. Every few weeks we bump into each other and every time I see her I admire her more.

I have asked her out three times, even sent her a letter with one thousand 'Pleases' on it but she either says 'No', or just ignores me. Although this might sound totally trivial to you, it is the most important thing in my life because I love her more and more each day.

Please help, you are my last chance. I saw her again at a firework party the other day and just don't know what to do. If you have ever loved anybody as much as I love her, you will understand.

Terence in Bexley is having more than girlfriend problems:

I need some advice urgently and when I saw *Growing Pains* I was inspired to write this letter. I have no one left to turn to. I had a few friends but they abandoned me when they discovered that I was having a heavy relationship with a 17-year-old-girl. She (I don't wish to disclose her name) is my only comfort now, but I fear that our relationship will soon come to an end. I don't know what I will do then. I have recently started smoking heavily and I fear for my health.

I have tried to think about suicide twice in the last three years but to no avail. I am forever having rows with my family and I feel depressed all the time.
Yours in desperation.

Peter in Sidcup also feels terrible:

My girlfriend and I are both 16 years old. We have been going out with each other for nearly a year now. The problem is that if she just glances at another boy I get jealous. I cannot help this. I daren't send for any leaflets through the post because if my post got intercepted by my mother or father I would die of embarrassment. I am ashamed of this feeling. I am also sure there are others like me.

And you're dead right about that! If I'm sure of one thing it is that most of the letters in this book represent the situations and feelings of thousands of other young people.

Michael (in Greenwich), for example, is stuck in a common state of mind (or heart). He is under exam pressure with all its stresses. He is feeling isolated and lonely. He glances at the TV screen and catches sight of someone who has powerful personal qualities of bravery and strength. He is moved. He falls in love. He knows nothing else about the person and has never said a word to her. But because he *needs* to believe the world has more bravery and strength in it than he dared to think possible, his emotions flare up. He is *in* love, showing all the correct symptoms. But he is *also* loving his own *need* because he recognises that the support of a loyal, powerful girl would make him feel better about almost everything. And this is not foolish – except that it's unlikely with this particular person since they are not acquainted.

I think, Michael, the thing to do is to recognise how very much you yearn for someone sincere to enter your life, how shy you feel about arranging this and how helpful it would be to try and share these feelings with people you *do* come into contact with, provided they appear grown-up enough to be able to sympathise. Again, by sharing your deeper feelings with people you give them the chance to do the same with you – just as a disaster at sea automatically reveals what people are made of underneath. You're hungry for a more 'spiritual' contact with others.

With Penny (in Sunderland), I am certain that things will also work out in the end. There's so much confidence in her letter that a boy is bound to fall for her personality soon. (PS – Nobody, but nobody, is put off because you wear glasses. Take it from one who wears glasses!)

Anne (in Southampton), you need to listen to your instincts. If the message you get on the surface is that your bloke loves you but somewhere inside he seems to be saying 'I'm just showing off a bit', then trust your feelings. After all, it's your feelings that count. Tell his lordship that you like him a lot but will wait and see how events turn out before giving him your complete commitment.

For Jennie (in Pulborough) I think the answer is that being chucked always feels horrible but perhaps you're better off without someone who doesn't seem to approve of you. As you say, you've got to be yourself, giggles and all, and it's fine to be like that anyway.

Cheryl (in Darlaston) could perhaps go back to her fella and tell him she thinks he's got a cheek to blame her for being silent when it takes at least *two* people *not* to hold a conversation. Obviously, he's at least equally tongue-tied, so don't take his verdict on you as anything like a sign of future doom. I'm sure you'll live to talk again and possibly with him. Remember, one battle is not the whole war.

For Nigel (in Wythenshawe) I think the problem is that you cannot really believe you have been chucked and there are two complications. First, there was never a proper explanation given as to why this relationship should end. Therefore you don't 'accept' it has happened. And second, you didn't really 'mourn your losses' when she did go off with another, but hid your feelings under that world-famous British stiff upper lip – 'Never mind, you'll get over her,' you said. I think you need to release some of your pain and anger. How dare she destroy all your hopes and dreams? What a waste! How awful it is to have someone treat you like an old cardigan! This is the way forward, since *she* is clearly not available to you anymore.

For Terence (in Bexley) the difficulty does not seem to be about one relationship going wrong but about all relationships failing, including those with your family. I think you should seek out a youth counselling service very quickly indeed, because the depression you've now got is quite strong.

Finally for Peter (in Sidcup), the problem also seems to be about your general situation rather than just the love affair. Apparently, at 16, you are not really confident that your parents would leave you to open your own letters. That must make you feel pretty insignificant in the scheme of things. And it's this feeling of insignificance that lies behind obsessively jealous behaviour. In a way, you are saying out loud, 'Anyone who goes out with me would really rather be going out with someone else.' If you felt confident about yourself, you wouldn't give two hoots if your girlfriend chatted to another boy. If you cannot have leaflets delivered at home (yet!), I suggest you read a book on self-assertion called *A Woman In Your Own Right* by Anne Dickson (published by Quartet). Don't worry that it's about women – you can apply all the lessons to yourself (as yet, there isn't a book on assertion training specifically for boys). That would help you, and so would talking intimately to your girlfriend in private about all the times you've felt overlooked, oppressed, second-best and unimportant. She will be attracted to you for risking yourself with her, rather than rejecting you as you fear.

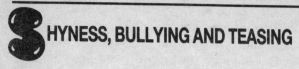

CHAPTER 7

SHYNESS, BULLYING AND TEASING

SHYNESS

Shyness is one of the biggest problems in your letters to *Growing Pains*. And yet when we're born, we're *not* shy – we learn to become so. A newborn baby is perfectly confident about making all the row in the world. It naturally demands attention and the satisfaction of all its needs.

Our shyness is almost always a response to our parents and how they behave. If they are backward in speaking up for themselves, or very tough when we ask for something, the result is that we learn to shut up. Being shy is a way of staying safe at home. Or it shows that we haven't been properly encouraged and accepted in the first place.

Shyness is *not* the same thing as being completely silent, however. A great number of show-offs are also shy. Many famous actors like Dirk Bogarde and Glenda Jackson have publicly confessed to being very shy. Many comedians are painfully unconfident when you meet them off the stage.

The dictionary defines shyness as being: 'easily frightened or startled', 'easily frightened away', 'difficult to approach', 'timid', 'over-cautious', 'frightened of meeting people', 'afraid of completing a task', 'cautiously reserved', 'shrinking from self-assertion', 'bashful'.

Are you shy? Yes, because everyone is, at least to begin with. We have to learn how to get on with other people. Animals are never shy. They have real fears. But shy people have all their fear locked inside them. They are afraid of – themselves. Are you? (Why? Think about it.) In the end: *You are shy – if you think you are.* Being shy stops you making friends, standing up for your rights, letting others see your good points. It makes you muddled, forgetful and unhappy. You imagine everyone is looking at you all the time. (It isn't true.)

Almost everyone who is shy is afraid of rejection. Usually, they have experienced a lot of rejection by other people. They have no confidence and don't want to be rejected again. But, instead of learning how to make others accept and like them, they shut the world out. They account for their isolation and shyness in terms of 'problems', usually about their appearance. I get hundreds of letters saying, 'the reason why I don't need to bother to try to make friends is because I am physically unacceptable, because I have spots, my ears stick out, I am bald, I am hairy, I am too short, too tall, I smell, I'm fat, I look like a girl/boy, I sweat, I stammer, I can't pee in a public toilet, I'm flat-chested, I'm half flat-chested, my nose is too big, my teeth are crooked and my shoulders are round.' I understand the misery people must be going through to say these things to me, but the fact is – we are all physically odd in some ways and even ugly people are attractive if they do the right things. The key is knowing how to shine *as a personality*, because that is what really establishes a friendship, not shape and looks which alter with time in any case. Many 'unattractive' people are actually *irresistible*!

Think about this. If you *were* suddenly made beautiful, your confidence might soar, but there is no guarantee of this because you still wouldn't know how to behave in the presence of others. It *always* has to be learned. *This is why many 'attractive' people are shy and lonely.*

We are all shy when asked to do something for the first time. We are all afraid of making fools of ourselves, until we realise that other people are only going to have a laugh and that won't kill us. In fact, if we are good sports, other people will *like* us for it. Generally, though, we cover up and avoid making the effort for quite a while. When it comes to dating, not many people want to be laughed at when they ask – although the laugh is really on the other person for being cruel and rude. Never give up, just because other people have something wrong with *them*! You must try again. Honesty is the best policy – say 'I've never done this before so I might make mistakes, but please help me.' You should *not* be punished for lack of experience. Miss Shy from Lincoln always punishes herself for lack of experience:

I am the world's most boring person and never go anywhere. I have no self-confidence and try not to talk to people. If anybody asks my opinion I try to find out what they think and agree with it. I couldn't possibly put my name on this letter but would say that if you have ever read *Little Miss Shy* in the Mister Men books, then you'll know who I am.

Angus in Renfrew says:

Dear Mr Hodson,
I am 14 years old and happy, except for the fact that certain people at school cannot help calling me U.G.L.Y. I know only too well that I am not exactly Marlon Brando, or even my Dad, when it comes to looks. I think I know what you are thinking: 'You don't know what U.G.L.Y. is.' I admit

I still have all my features and nothing missing but I feel completely unimportant. I only have to get into an argument with someone and they say the dreaded word.

I used to be the most confident person you could ever meet. Now I am very retiring and will not approach new people. I don't suffer from bad acne or anything like that. The worst of it is that my best friend is very handsome – he has girls swarming around him. A girl only has to see me and she screams.

You may think I am feeling sorry for myself. In reality, it is my self-confidence that is suffering, and suffering quite badly. People used to tell me to be quiet and they'd say 'Shut up, chatterbox.' Now I won't talk and am reluctant to make friends.

I am told I have a good personality. But what does that matter if nobody will look at me?

Ian in Peebles is also worried about his appearance:

I couldn't possibly go out with a girl because my body is triangular-shaped. I am 14 and surely I shouldn't have shoulders that slope downwards and be wider at the hips than I am across the chest? No one will want me.

Jack in Frinton writes:

I am not a shy person but I am very much in love with a girl at a well-known private school near here who seems to lack confidence. I know from another friend that she likes me but she hasn't been able to talk to me directly.

I wonder whether you would be able to mention this on your programme so that her problem of shyness would no longer keep us apart. I am sure that if I approached her directly she would simply die of embarrassment. Hope you will do this for love.

And this is from Gerry in Scarborough:

I am writing to you in the hope of getting some advice.

When I see an item of clothing in a shop like Concept Man or Burton's, I can never pluck up enough courage to go in and buy it. Every time I try to go into a shop I come over hot. I always think the attendants in there are thinking – 'Nothing in this shop would ever suit him!'

I am 15 years old and my Mum buys all my clothes for me. Please could you give me some advice?

And from Miss Anonymous, aged 8½:

I am shy about going to a different school because I won't know anybody. I cannot get over it. I feel embarrassed when I cannot jump in with the skipping-rope.

And from Gloria in Pagham:

Please help me. I'm nearly 16 and I'm leaving school in June. My problem is that I always think I'm not good enough to do anything. I feel that when someone is looking at me they're thinking how horrible and useless I am. This is making me feel very depressed. I sit in my bedroom and cry for hours. I don't even like to be seen in public. I stay in all the time.

I've taken my CSE exams and my results will be coming in June. I'm so upset because I don't think anyone will want me to work for them. I only want to work in a small shop, selling things, but I hate myself so much. I've talked to my Mum and she said I would grow out of it. I won't. It gets worse every day. I've tried to get advice from mags but I've never been answered. Please, please, please help me. I hate myself and just want to hide away from everyone.

Bonny from Milton Keynes has a different type of shyness:

I watched your programme on shyness and you mentioned people who couldn't talk because of it. My problem is completely opposite – I cannot stop talking because of it. You see, if a boy comes to talk to me, instead of going quiet I chat like mad. I think it's because I don't want them to go away and leave me on my own. Because if they do, I have to go through it all again. And when I chat about nothing, it puts them off completely.

   Please sort me out.

Jean in West Sussex says:

I have two problems that lots of my friends have trouble with. The first one is that we feel embarrassed to ask boys to parties and to go to boys' parties. How do we stop getting embarrassed? My other problem is that when the hairdresser combs my hair he scrapes my ears and I have not got enough pluck to tell him. What should I do about these problems?

Margaret in York is troubled about blushing:

I was really pleased to hear that you will be discussing shyness on *Growing Pains* this Saturday. I suffer from being shy and it makes me feel really miserable because I can't be myself when I'm with other people. I find BLUSHING a great problem. I am so self-conscious that if anyone starts talking to me I start to blush. I keep thinking everybody's watching me all the time. I have seen advertisements in a few local papers about hypnotism for blushing and self-confidence. I am writing to ask you whether you think it's worth trying.
Yours hopefully.

Joy in Aston writes:

Dear *Growing Pains*,
I'm 12 years old and madly in love. He's 5 foot 10, very handsome and popular. Although he is in the same year as me, I do not know him very well. He's different from the rest and I know he'd really like me if we just got to know each other. But there's a problem. I am too shy to ask him

out. I am not really a shy person and I have lots of boys as friends.

My friends have been very encouraging and helpful which has been nice. I am quite tall (5 foot 5) and quite attractive too, but I am desperate to know what I should do.

Love from his love-sick fan.

(PS – His name is ———— ————!)

And there are loads more letters along the same lines, many of them from people in their late teens and twenties. (I also get letters from people in *all* age groups – up to ages 50 or 60 – about this problem, so it's not a minor one nor a childish one.) How can shyness be dealt with then?

First, try to realise that you cannot be blamed for the way you feel. It is not your fault if you've learned to be *too* quiet (or *too* talkative) at home (where it keeps you out of trouble) and yet this does *not* serve you well in the outside world. The sensible thing to do is to accept that when going outside your home you may need a different type of skill, language and behaviour. Meeting strangers, after all, is different from seeing your relatives.

Being successful with new people requires different ways of talking, listening and looking. You also have to practise these skills, perhaps with 'safe' people to begin with – shopkeepers, librarians, swimming-bath cashiers, telephone operators – people with whom it doesn't really matter if you get a bit tongue-tied.

Shy people have very 'stiff' faces. They don't use the muscles of their eyes, mouths or foreheads very much when talking or (above all) listening. The major problem with shy people is that by keeping their heads down, their voices low, their eyes away from others and their faces frozen into a mask *they don't appear shy but cold*! Other people actually think *you* are rejecting *them*. One very good way to 'loosen up' is to *take your face for a jog*. What you do is sit in front of the mirror and practise saying 'me/you/me/you/me/you/me/you' quite loud, lots of times over to get those facial muscles working. Also, practise doing ultra-slow exaggerated smiles as another muscle exercise.

How do you chat up a girl or boy? I've received several hundred letters beginning 'I don't know what to say . . .' Well, there *isn't* a script. You can't learn a series of catchphrases and gags. The only rules are: a) take a deep breath b) look the person in the eye, don't stare at the floor c) smile d) be friendly and interested in *them*. Then you will know what to say, because you *ask them about themselves*. It's better to put general questions like 'How are you?' 'What have you been doing?' 'Tell me about yourself', than questions which get a simple 'Yes' or 'No' such as 'Do you like A?' Never start by talking about yourself – 'I like it here but my left leg's playing me up a bit' says a lot about you but nothing to interest anyone else as yet. Speak slowly and very clearly. Do not mumble. Listening is done with the *eyes* first and the *ears* second. Keep looking at the person. Nod and say 'Mmm' during pauses. Say 'Yes' when people ask 'Do you know what I mean?' Show that you have heard people by getting it straight – 'You think it's OK to do it this way, do you?' is the sort of thing you can say. Don't give orders. Saying 'Don't you think . . .' in fact means 'Don't think', and people don't like it.

Apathy (or inactivity) often follows from shyness because you get isolated. Don't sleep till noon or watch telly till midnight, then go back to bed. You need to go out, if only to volunteer for unpaid work at the local old people's home or play sport, since exercise cheers you up and you are more likely to make new friends if you get out and about. Your local reference library can help you with any enquiries about activities like these. Or you could join a youth club in the area.

So, what's the cure? Shyness vanishes as soon as you start to realise that other people are not watching you – they are actually worried about what you think of them! Nobody can really know what's going on in your head unless you tell them, so there's really no need to feel self-conscious. It's all right – you are safe! As soon as you smile and start to talk, people will respond. But if you believe they are laughing at you (when they are not), your face will appear flushed and suspicious. Then people will really think that *you* don't like *them*!! Shy people who go on looking shy can't make friends because they do not invite confidence from others. One of the most helpful things you can do in an awkward situation is to draw attention to your shyness because it instantly puts others at ease and they stop seeing you as cold. Just say 'I feel a bit shy here.' Their behaviour will then make you feel more comfortable, especially as *no one* can now accuse you of . . . being shy. You've turned a supposed 'weakness' into a strength.

And so, 'Miss Shy' (in Lincoln), it is by no means true that you are the world's most boring person. That is your defence against having to meet new people. You will quickly discover that people can be much more boring than you if you put into practice the talking techniques I've just suggested! The basic point remains true for Angus (in Renfrew) and Ian (in Peebles). For Jack (from

Frinton) the most helpful thing to understand would be that – however shy his 'girlfriend' might be, he is even *more* shy. What! you want me to chat her up on your behalf and act as a go-between? Perish the thought! Nor would it solve your problem – even in 'arranged marriages' there comes the fateful day when the two parties actually have to speak to each other. Her potential embarrassment is not *your* responsibility. If you want to ask her out, you have only to do so and *she* has the choice of saying 'Yes' or 'No' (or dying of shame. And I know that won't happen either). I have the same advice for Joy in Aston.

For Gerry (in Scarborough) I have every possible sympathy, as I share the problem myself. I feel dreadful in those shops where fairly snotty assistants come up to you as soon as you've walked through the door, eye you up and down and ask you what on earth they can do for you! (My ideal shop would have no 'assistants' at all, just people on the tills at the exit.) The answer, I found, was to experiment by degrees. To start with, just go into shops, look round and come out again without risking a purchase. Get comfortable with the business of being in a shop. Then, when you feel more at ease, ask the odd question about this or that item. Hold clothes up to your body and look at yourself in the mirrors. Eventually, you'll be able to try things on. Remember – this kind of shopping is always easier to manage if you go with a friend.

For 'Miss Anonymous', the answer's this. Changing schools *is* difficult, so you'll definitely need some help. Tell Mum and Dad about your worries. Ask them to ask the school if there's someone living near you who already goes there, who could show you around for the first few days. As for skipping, offer to *hold* the rope. Tell the girl skipping how good she is at it (if she's OK) and say 'I wonder how you do that?' I bet she'll tell you, and show you and help you.

For Gloria (in Pagham) the answer is to see a youth counsellor because you have become very depressed about exams, leaving school (and your friends), starting work and feeling unlovable. This is the time of life that almost everybody finds difficult and there's no need to be ashamed to ask for a hand. If there's nothing near you in Pagham, contact the London Youth Advisory Service, 26 Prince of Wales Road, London NW5 (telephone 01-267 4792) and pay them a visit. (I also suggest that you read Fiona's letter at the end of this section.)

For Jean (in West Sussex) the answer is to rehearse what you mean to say before you have to say it. Work out what you're going to say to the boys and the hairdresser. You could even 'role-play' – get a friend to pretend to be the hair-stylist while you sit in a chair and say in an authoritative voice, 'Please don't comb my ears – it hurts. I don't like it.' I assure you the response you get in the salon will be apologetic and not angry because they want to stay in business.

Bonny's talkativeness is caused by anxiety. She could do with some relaxation exercises to build her confidence so that she doesn't always interrupt but listens as well as talks. She could send off for some tapes of exercises from Lifeskills (address given on the next page).

Margaret (from York) is troubled by blushing, as indeed are many others. This is another of those problems (like panics) where you *react* to your own reactions. We all have a blushing *system* – it's part of our fear/anger response. Blood is carried to the surface of the skin to cool us down. If you just let it happen, it lasts for seconds and often not long enough for others to notice. If you *mistakenly* think blushing means that someone else can share every embarrassing thought you've got in your head, you will prolong the blush. You have got to give yourself permission to make mistakes instead of seeking to be perfect. Do an experiment with your friends. Ask *them* about blushing – if they ever do it and what it feels like. Then say you want to try to blush and get them to describe what you look like when you do. By 'confessing' in this way, I doubt if you'll even be able to blush. If you do, you'll be surprised at how little impact it has on others, compared with the enormous effect it has on you.

Books on how to cope with shyness are published by the Sheldon Press, Marylebone Road, London NW1 4DU. Write for their catalogue in the Overcoming Common Problems series. In the public library, you might be able to find *Shyness* by Philip Zimbardo (originally published by Pan books in 1977) which is very helpful. Tapes on building self-confidence and assertiveness are available from Lifeskills, 3 Brighton Road, London N2. Send a stamped addressed envelope for current list and prices.

Before we leave shyness, let's hear from Fiona in Birmingham:

Dear *Growing Pains*,
I am writing about shyness – all through my school life, until last May/June, I used to be shy. I was ignored by everyone, except when someone wanted something. Then I'd drop everything to do what they wanted. I suppose I was looking for *any* attention.

This all changed last May when I had my exams and left

school to do my revision. I was a bit overweight, so my Mum suggested some activity to lose weight. I had always wanted to go weight-training but never had the nerve to do it.

So one day my Mum took me to the swimming baths which had weight-training for women. I was very shy and was not enjoying myself but as I started working out I began to lose my tension – and my weight.

Now I go weight-training every day. I go to college and I am really enjoying myself. I have good friends and I am taking part in the lessons. I am really looking forward to going out to find a job when I leave college.

They say that the school years are supposed to be the most enjoyable. Well, to me they were the worst. They made me depressed sometimes. I even thought it would be best if I wasn't alive at all. Now I am looking forward to my future. Everyone I have known for a long time says that I look much better and some cannot believe the change. Comments like that make everybody enjoy life.

(PS – It doesn't have to be weight-training!)

BULLYING

I am including letters on bullying and teasing in the shyness chapter for the simple reason that they do go together. Shy people are usually unassertive. They get picked on. They can't stand teasing. They often fall victim to bullies. This is not their 'fault' – it's a fact and there's a reason for it. Bullies are made angry *by* shy people because inside, bullies are really afraid that *they* are shy and weak and *they cannot bear to see the connection*. So they beat it up.

Mrs Griggs writes from Bournemouth:

For months, my 10-year-old son complained of illness and wouldn't go to school. I eventually found out that he was being bullied by a gang from the comprehensive school on his journey. I reported this to the headmaster, the boys were disciplined and the problem stopped.

But now it seems to have started once again. My son is desperately unhappy and has pleaded with me not to report the bullies who have threatened to do all sorts of things to him if he tells. How would you advise me to tackle this situation?

People also get picked on for being 'different', as the letter from Colin in Petersfield shows:

I am 13 years old and have been bullied my whole school life. In my primary school, it was because I lived in a better area of Epping and I was quite chubby. So when I moved to secondary school, I made sure it was quite a way away so nobody knew me, and I had lost some weight. I love the school I now go to, but the bullying has got worse. Because I am good in school and I get good grades, most of the boys in my class (and some of the girls) hate me. One of the boys has taken it so far that when I walk downstairs, he kicks me in the back of the knees so I fall over. Outside the drama hut, he throws stones at me and the other boys join in. I do not like thinking about this subject but when you mentioned it I felt I had to.

A bully is someone who makes him or herself 'a terror to the weak or undefended'. As I said, almost all bullies feel weak on the inside and almost all bullies can get frightened too. A strong person does not need to bully anyone, whereas a bully often feels inferior.

Having said that, *some* bullies are merely rough kids whose families behave like that and have lots of fights and squabbles. This boisterous behaviour may still frighten quieter children (and some grown-ups too). Real bullies, however, may not *know* how to make friends. They just find that frightening someone is less lonely for them than having no contact with anyone. They 'make themselves feel better by making others feel worse'. A bully may be very unhappy at home. A bully may be jealous of other kids in his or her family and therefore jealous of *all* similar children. A bully may be under stress.

Having explained that, how can you defend yourself against the knuckle sandwich?

- Tell someone reliable exactly what is going on. Occasionally, just talking about that dratted Dougie Pratmouth is enough.
- Sometimes you need to get your parents or teachers to take action. *This is not sneaking, since it's always wrong to keep secrets that screw you up*.
- If possible, find allies. There are usually more people on your side and no bully is prepared to tackle a big group.
- Let the bully know you *will* tell. When he or she taunts you with 'Tell tale tit, your tongue will split', reply – 'Well that's better than being bullied by you, at any rate.'

Being bullied can be like living in a vicious circle, so you need help getting out of it. *The Willow Street Kids* by Michelle Eliot (published by Deutsch) is a very good book for explaining these ideas further.

And so Mrs Griggs, the only thing you can do is find out what your son has been threatened with, and take the severest possible action, including police prosecutions if there have been menacing threats of assault. If you don't respond to that part of your son that has told you about his problem, you are teaching him that 'might is right', that 'bullying is fine' and parents don't care. Involve *both* schools at once (your son's and the comprehensive) and make sure he's safe – perhaps keeping him at home until the matter has been dealt with. No headteacher willingly tolerates bullying and you will be supported.

As for Colin (in Petersfield), I think the best advice comes in two other letters, the first from Carol in Surrey:

During my time at secondary school, I was bullied on several occasions. Most of the time people were picking on me about my looks, but what could I do about *them*? I often felt I really wanted to talk to somebody about what bullies had done to me inside, but for a long time I couldn't.

Bullying, by the way, is not clever – it is a coward's way of impressing friends. If you are impressed by this you are as cold and mean as the person doing the bullying. People who bully deserve no respect and should be punished.

Above all if you are being bullied, don't hold it inside. Tell someone, a teacher perhaps. In the end I did. It is most important to talk about your feelings and experiences with someone else. You'll probably find that most people have come across this problem for themselves. I solved my problem and the bullying stopped. I hope it will for you.

And this from Angie in Beckenham:

Just over 2 years ago I was being bullied by two girls who were 4 years older than I was. I didn't dare go out at all. They came to my school and my home. This torment lasted for 8 months. Suddenly, instead of feeling scared for myself I decided to stand up for myself. One day the girls went for me and I fought back. After that, they never touched me again. I'd just like to tell others that even if you think the bullies are tougher than you, you should defend yourself.

To which I would only add that self-defence does not always have to include fighting. Your biggest weapon is your brain. I got bullied when I was a fat teenager by a boy called Malcolm Roberts. One day I realised that he kept on going for me because he was plump too (although taller and stronger). I told him about this great new diet I was going on that was bound to work and help *anyone* lose weight. He got interested and wanted to know what the diet was. Suddenly, he needed me. And when he started relating to me as a useful source of information, do you know he forgot to thump me?

TEASING

Teasing is a kind of verbal bullying and many of the same rules and lessons apply. 'S' from Avon writes:

I have a big problem. When I am at school I am called 'Samantha Fox' – because I'm big on top. My Mum says it's how I'm made. When we do cross-country, my PE kit shows that I am big. Please help.
(PS – I mean that I have a big bust.)

Claire, aged 10, writes from Worcester:

I have a problem. My friends call me 'Hitler' because I was born in Germany. They say where you're born is what you are. I don't believe that because my Mum is Scottish and my Dad is English so I must be a mixture of both. I was born in Germany because my Mum and Dad were in the British army there. So I'm not German am I?

'Mickey Mouse' in Cheshire writes:

Dear *Growing Pains*,
I have got MASSIVE ears. Please, please, please can you help?
Yours desperately (and anonymously)
Mickey Mouse of Cheshire
(PS – If you do read this out please do not mention where I come from. Thank you.)

He adds, 'Don't take this as a joke – it's certainly not for me. The picture is not quite accurate but it's not far off.'

'Unnamed of Kent' has a similar sort of problem:

I'm writing to you because I have got a big nose. At school I get called lots of names like 'Captain Beaky' and 'Pinnochio' etc. I try to ignore them, but I can't.

Is there any way I can disguise the size of my nose with make-up or by wearing my hair in a certain way?

Even my family and friends make fun of the size of my nose and I get really upset. Please help me. I am 14.

Sheila from Portsmouth says:

I am Sheila and I'm 11 years old. I am having a lot of trouble at school with all my friends. The reason, I am embarrassed to say, is that I haven't any real knowledge of the latest fashions and pop music and that sort of thing. At school, every half-term or something like that, we have 'mufti days' when we can wear whatever we want instead of uniform. I go to school in what I think might be fashionable but all my friends tease me. And I'm frightened to say what pop group or songs I like because I know they'll tease me about that too. Have you got any suggestions? I want to keep my friends, though.

Pamela writes from Stevenage:

I am writing about the bullying that Sarah Greene mentioned. There is a group of girls in my class who are constantly bullying me. They have no reason at all for it. At the beginning of term, my Mum cut down a bib-fronted pinafore into a skirt and a girl in my class said 'Poor her – Mummy can't afford a new skirt.' I was really hurt by this. Then they started saying things to my friend Hilary. For instance, they told her I was laughing about her new beret, which is a lie. They are also saying despicable things to my other friend Michaela, like 'If you speak to her, I won't speak to you.' The thing that gets me is that the ring-leader's Mum is a social worker. I really don't know who to turn to, and it is depressing me. A couple of Fridays ago, I was taking my dog for a walk and she accidentally nipped a 'toughie' in my class who went and told her Mum. Her Mum came to my door and lied, saying the dog was off the lead. She said I told the dog to bite her daughter. My Mum and Dad are separated, which I think adds to the problem, *and* my Mum is off work and going into hospital on Wednesday.

Frances in Surrey is just 12:

I have a really agonising problem. I've just started secondary school and I've found that I'm allergic to two of my teachers – they make me sneeze. It would be fine if I sneezed like a normal person, but I sneeze like a chi-hua-hua puppy! And the whole school knows it. There is a particular group of people who make fun of me. My parents tell me to ignore them, but when I do they start kicking me and shouting at me. When I say something, they do exactly the same thing. And my friends just walk off and leave me to my fate. If you have any advice, I'm open to suggestions.

Joey in Southend says:

I'm writing for your advice because about a year ago I decided I wanted to become a vegetarian. My Mum and step-Dad didn't mind at the time because they thought it wouldn't last, but they were wrong, 'cos I still am.

My problem is that every time we sit down to dinner they start saying things to me like 'Oh look at this pork chop I'm eating, it used to be a pig running round . . .' How can I get them to stop?

Jenny in Faversham says:

Dear Phillip,
I have got quite a pale skin. This never used to worry me, but recently these boys have been calling me 'junkie' and 'druggie'. I have tried fake tan but it looks like I've got mud on my face. Please help, but don't say my name on TV.
Jenny

How can you stop being teased? The first and most obvious fact to take on board is this: at some time, for whatever reason, it *is* going to happen. You cannot stop the world from taking the mickey out of you if it wants to. People will call you names and the only choice you have is about *how and whether you react*. If something is inevitable, the best thing to do is to be prepared for it.

How then do you get prepared for ridicule? The answer is obvious. By predicting what sorts of things are likely to be said about you. By rehearsing in your own mind how you feel about these things. And by telling yourself the truth about them, so you *cannot* be ambushed.

For example, if you *are* overweight, some unkind idiot at some point is going to call you 'fatty'. OK, so be it. How do *you* feel about being overweight? Do you understand why it has happened to you? Do you say to yourself, 'I'll lose weight when I want to', or 'I'm happy being heavy so who cares!' or do you pretend you're not fat and get angry with everyone who says you are? Which is the more sensible course to follow?

Do you think that you have real skills and talents or do you imagine you've achieved nothing? If you haven't made much effort in life, is teasing going to be harder for you to take or not? Can you control the teaser? No, as we've said. Could you feel better about yourself by playing a sport, finding a hobby, helping in the family, earning some pocket money, joining a club, going camping, learning a musical instrument? Answer – 'Yes you could.' That's the way you can reduce the *power* of the teaser and that is the only way, apart from arming yourself with this idea: *Every teaser finally gets bored if you don't respond*.

That's what 'S' (from Avon) needs to know. I appreciate, 'S', that having a big bust is no joke. It can be very painful, especially when you first develop. Your breasts can be sore and their weight can give you backache. They make you so self-conscious that you think you'll die with embarrassment. You also run the risk of becoming distinctly round-shouldered. Alas, you cannot choose your physical size. Some girls begin breast-growth at 9 and are full size when they're 12. You don't tell me your actual age – but someone in your class had to be first and it's you. Soon, lots of your friends will join you and develop what the Duchess of York calls an 'Up Top', making you feel less conspicuous. By the time you're 14 you may even enjoy your shape – though I am told no woman ever feels

100 per cent happy with her boobs. If you get very, very big – you can think about a possible 'breast reduction' operation when your body is fully grown. In the meantime, always wear a bra and don't settle for a cheapo.

For Claire (in Worcester), the fact is that you are a British citizen of British stock. The British Army of the Rhine, as it's called, is only *in* Germany because it helped to beat Hitler in 1945. If you wanted, you could apply for a passport and show your friends you're as British as roast beef – but that's only playing into their hands. I suggest you deal with it by making fun of their teasing. At a suitable moment, announce 'Ve haff ways of coping with you British!'

For 'Mickey Mouse', I'm glad that you can half-joke about what is a real problem. It means you are well-adjusted already, and in fact your GP can do the rest. About one in 200 people suffer from protruding ears. Even Prince Charles has the problem and a lot of women have liked him, not just because his Mum was Queen. Strapping them back with plaster doesn't help. You can grow your hair longer. But a simple operation to take a tuck behind your ears can change their position and 'fold your wings' back into the customary position parallel to the sides of your head. You'll need 1 to 2 days in hospital and there will be no visible scars. (A note for others: this operation is not performed before the patient is 5 years of age.) As a result of mentioning your sort of problem on TV, I've had lots of letters from viewers who've solved their problem in this way.

Perhaps 'Unnamed of Kent' also needs to take medical advice to see whether relief could come in the form of a plastic surgery operation? There's little else you can do to hide a huge nose, although cosmetic camouflage information can be found in the chapter on Spots and blemishes.

Sheila (in Portsmouth) could very easily help herself. First, realise it is OK to be different sometimes. Not everyone likes pop music and if you really loathe it, don't pretend otherwise. However, if you wish to be in the swing, you can always watch programmes like *Going Live*. Watch the fashions; listen to the groups. Read magazines like *Smash Hits* and get clued up. Then when it's your turn to talk, you'll have lots to contribute and will even be able to tell your friends when *they* are out of fashion.

For Pamela (in Stevenage), I think half the trouble is that you're worried by what's happening to your family and feeling very sensitive to any criticism, particularly of your Mum. You need a cuddle and someone to support you. Can your Dad do this, or an aunt? You may not see so much of your father, but he remains your Dad and I hope he'd listen to your troubles and cheer you up if you asked him. Let's hope things will get better when your Mum has her health back. There's nothing to be ashamed of in not wasting money on new skirts when someone is as clever as your Mum and can turn 'old' into 'new'. I wonder whether *their* Mums could do it.

For Frances (in Surrey), the important thing to decide is how disruptive you're being. Sneezing happens when it's dusty or to clear our noses, or when we are very excited, nervous, worried or generally aroused. It's a reflex clearance of our nasal tubes with a blast of air. I'm sure it's huge fun for these people to set you off. But if it's just six or seven sneezes, shrug it off – it's not your fault. If the *teachers* complain to you, however, saying something has *got* to be done, then see your doctor.

For Joey (in Southend), the answer is to help your parents with *their* problem. Tell them that lots of famous and long-lived people are vegetarian and these days more people than ever before eat no meat. Tell them you like it – it suits you, and surely they want you to feel happy? Tell them their teasing is getting on your nerves but that you won't tease them back for eating meat. In fact, you're perfectly happy to live and let live and are definitely *not* criticising them for what they consume, nor trying to convert them to eating grass, nor rejecting their love by wanting different food. This last point is very important. Say you love them very much but are beginning to lose respect for them, so can they please give over?

Finally, for Jenny (in Faversham), I suggest the answer to your difficulty lies in this letter from Brendan in Immingham:

Dear Agony Uncle,
May I make a suggestion? A few years ago I read a good idea for coping with teasing. I was (and still am) a bit overweight and was teased, so I know what it's like.

Write down a list of names that you could possibly be called and carry it around with you and if someone calls you something, you can check your list. If the word's there, no problem. Give it a tick. If it's not, you can say 'Great, I've got another name to add to my collection!' The teasing will soon die down.

I only wish I had known of this idea for turning the tables on teasers when I was at school. I hope it's helpful.

And so do I.

CHAPTER 8

SPOTS AND BLEMISHES

I think this is one subject most adults no longer understand – how miserable you can feel when your face is patrolled by a fleet of red and white bumps all looking for somewhere noticeable to park themselves. Spots. Acne. Zits. You name it, it's embarrassing and shy-making. What adults usually say is meant well enough but hopeless. Something along the lines of – 'Don't worry. They'll definitely be gone by the time you're 26!' To a person of 14, that's half a lifetime away.

Your teens are a time when you want to look your best and because you've got spots you fear you may look your worst. You are self-conscious because you need to become the *real you* – no longer just a part of Mum, Dad and the family. You identify with them less and with your own age group more. This feels *competitive.* And your *outer* appearance has to work overtime because you may not have too much inner confidence to call on. Part of you does not want to make much effort anyway and will seize on any excuse – like spots – to avoid making friends and going out. When we talked about spots on the television, we got thousands of letters. Here are a few, starting with Michele, from Wimbledon:

I have a lot of spots and I'm fed up with squeezing them and wasting my money on spot stuff which doesn't work.

And Frankie in Newbury:

I am 14 years old and have a bad problem with spots. I go to a mixed school and get called horrible names like 'beanface'. Even my best friend calls me these names and now she tells my other so-called friends to call me them as well. It is very depressing and I often feel like crawling under a stone and not coming out. There is no one I can talk to except you on *Growing Pains*. I envy all the girls in my class who have boyfriends. I think spots are the reason why I am the only one who hasn't. No boy has ever asked me out in my life. I've tried to talk to my Mum and she just says 'Don't worry, they'll go away.' But they don't. A spot concealer would never cover them. I am probably the ugliest girl in the school.

And from Boy in Hertfordshire:

Please could you help me? I am so embarrassed to go swimming because I have got spots on my chest and back.

And from Natalie in Southport:

I am nearly 14 and have quite a lot of spots on my face, chest and back. I have been to the doctor's and I was told that I have acne on my back and the beginnings of acne on my chest. What is so annoying is that my friends get hardly any spots at all. I have tried Clearasil which did not help much and I have also tried Biactol which left my skin all dry with a patch of dry red skin that looked worse. What do you suggest?

And from David in Hull:

I am a 16-year-old boy and quite good-looking apart from having about nineteen spots on my face, with a new one appearing almost every week. In the past 6 months, I've been out with two girls and each relationship lasted only 2 to 3 weeks – then they finished with me, due to my complexion. I avoid going out as much as I can. I feel like locking myself away so that people cannot see me. Please help. All I want is a clear complexion.

And also Anon in Derbyshire:

I don't know what age *Growing Pains* is for, but I am 15 years old and towards the end of my O-level studies. My spots have been part of my life since my fourth year in the juniors, when I was 10 or 11. It started off with just one or two, but now I have between twenty and forty every single day. You may be thinking, 'God, does she count them?' The answer to that is 'Yes!' I have got so worked up about them that not only have I stayed in when my friends have gone to the cinema or a weekly disco, but I have also started missing school. In fact, I am writing this letter at 9.20 am on a Monday morning and I should be at school right now.

I have tried all the products to get rid of them – Biactol, Oxy 5, Oxy 10, TCP, Clearasil, etc. I have also been to my doctor's. She put me on a course of antibiotics and when I went back because they had not gone, she said 'Come on then, let's have a look at THE SPOT.' I was very upset by this attitude and have not been back since.

I have saved up and bought a facial sauna which, although it does wonders for your skin, does not help get rid of spots. What makes me really mad is that my friends actually lie to me when they're trying to cheer me up, saying – 'What spots?' or 'You can't see them', when I know damned well you can. People keep telling me that others have much worse spots than me, which is true, but how does that help *me* to get rid of *my* spots?

People say 'You will soon grow out of them.' How much longer? Another 10 years! It's like a prison sentence. I don't know why I'm writing because you can't help me or any other sufferers at all. Sorry for

wasting your time.
(PS – No kid will ever know what pain they cause when they tease a 'zitty' person, until they get spots themselves.)

OK, let's hold the anger for a minute and look at some of the facts. Common acne, as it's called, can make you feel the way a leper felt 100 years ago: shunned and persecuted. Yet acne *is* common – over 70 per cent of all teenagers get some acne spots so we have to say this *curse* is a *normal* part of growing up.

You get acne cysts because, as you start to mature and your body chemistry changes, your skin makes more of a special oily fat called 'sebum'. This clogs up your pores where the hairs grow, making a plug. More sebum is pushed upwards but cannot escape to the surface – it's a bit like a strongly capped oil-well. A bump appears and the rubbish in the hole starts to get infected and begins to decay. Your body attacks the decay with its own defence cells and the end result is a white and red inflamed pressure point on your face, neck and chest where your largest sebum glands exist.

How can you treat the trouble? One golden answer is: *not quickly*. I'll repeat that in case you didn't get the point: *acne cannot be cleared up overnight*. First, decide if your affliction is 'mild' or 'heavy'. To do this, compare yourself with your friends (a dodgy business, I realise, since you think your problem is the worst in the world). If you think you've just got the mild version, then try self-help remedies. Experiment with the products you *can* buy at the chemist. See if your skin likes them. But carry out the instructions on the tube or packet and keep applying the cream for several weeks. You cannot hope to get much of a result inside about 2 months. So when Michele and Natalie and Anon in Derbyshire say these treatments don't work, I seriously question how long they tried them for.

If you have a great army of spots and the covering is extensive, visit your GP who can give you tablets and antibiotic creams, peeling agents and astringents. However, again, don't expect a real result inside two or three months. The sooner you go for treatment, the fewer scars you'll have afterwards. Don't pick or squeeze spots unless you really can't help doing it. First off, everyone's fingers are pretty filthy and most of the dirt is right under the nails, waiting to make your skin infections worse. Second, the spot is just as likely to implode (inwards) as explode (outwards) and the infection will go deeper into your flesh. If you must 'go gardening' (as I used to call it) then go to the chemist and get an 'extractor' which you can keep sterile.

Here are some more facts about acne:

● The spots are not infectious to others.
● They don't indicate that you are 'run down'.
● They don't 'run in families'.
● They are not caused by 'nerves', although being nervous about having them might make you a picker.
● They don't mean you are dirty – washing doesn't help and may make your skin even more sore, so tell that to Granny!
● Sunshine helps but don't overdose.
● Sunbeds are not recommended.
● Cosmetics may make spots worse by putting fresh grease into the pores.

- The black in blackheads is *not* dirt, it is skin pigment.
- Anti-bacterial lotion helps.
- Sex doesn't cause spots (or every grown-up would have them).
- Food does not cause spots or make them better. Life with acne is miserable enough without blaming yourself for eating the wrong things. (Scientists did an experiment with chocolate, for example, and stuffed some lucky kids in a Willy Wonker-type chocolate room till they couldn't eat another bar. Their spots did not get worse – but they did feel sick.) The fat and grease in your skin is *not* the fat you eat – it's made in the skin.
- Most spots will go by the time you're 26 (big deal, I know).
- People notice your spots much *less* than you do because you value your looks much *more* than they do.
- Nobody was ever a perfect 10, anyway.
- There are *no* miracle cures. But 70 per cent of all cases of acne, if properly treated, will improve after 8 weeks.

And so, Anon in Derbyshire, back to you. Part of your problem is that you don't have acne as such. You have a version called 'picker's acne'. Most of your spots are there because you prod and poke every little blemish in your skin. I don't blame you for this. I simply wonder what all your other stresses and tensions are about. Life does seem to be getting a bit on top of you and you're very sensitive to rejection and teasing. Yes, we all hate rejection and teasing, I agree. But your use of sarcasm and the bunking off from school seem to say that you're pretty depressed. I don't think anybody listens to you much when you get upset generally and that may be why you get so obsessed with your appearance. I have no magic answer for that – I just know that if you could start talking to someone reliable about your troubles, you would feel a lot better. And you'd have fewer spots.

If there's no one in the family, is there a counselling service attached to your school? If not, ask at your local Citizen's Advice Bureau (they are in the telephone directory) about the nearest Youth Advisory Service. They can help. And if you (or any other readers) want specific advice about any type of acne, you can take part in a free skincare survey organised by the Acnidazil Company, which includes a questionnaire. Write to Acnidazil Survey, Burson-Marstelier, 24–28 Bloomsbury Way, London WC1A 2PX for your copy. If you still have acne in your late teens, ask your GP whether the drug 'Diane' would be helpful. Let's leave the last word on acne to Denise in Essex:

Dear *Growing Pains*,
When I heard you were going to talk about spots I thought I'd write and tell you about my experiences.

Ever since the age of 12, I've suffered from some kind of skin trouble, be it spots, acne, dry skin, blackheads or blemishes. But I've come through them all. Sometimes, my spots got so bad that I wouldn't go out but now I've learnt that it's no good shutting yourself away – because other people are suffering from the same problems around you. Also, people never see your spots in the same way as you do. Spot sufferers are always more conscious of their problem but the only way others can begin to tell how bad it is, is if you pick them.

I can't say I've got a clear complexion now because I haven't, but I never sit by and let people take the mickey

SPOTS AND BLEMISHES 113

out of me. Instead, I laugh with them and even make fun of myself sometimes. I am now 14.

There are also one or two letters about other skin problems, like this one from Mrs Levinson in Canterbury:

My son of 11 has a port-wine stain birthmark over his right cheek. We've always tried to accept it as one of those things but now he's becoming much more aware of his appearance and I promised to see if there was anything we could do about it. Can you help?

Yes. Happily this red stain is harmless although it is permanent. Surgery is sometimes helpful but carries a risk of scarring, and that would not be an improvement. The best results are obtained by using 'skin camouflage'. This technique is practised at a few hospitals and some salons. It is relatively new but very effective and not expensive. Write for details to Thomas Blake and Company, Blatchford Close, Horsham, Sussex RH13 5RQ. A similar service is offered via The British Red Cross Society, Beauty Care Organiser, 9 Grosvenor Crescent, London SW1X 7EJ.

Roberta in Gravesend writes:

Dear *Growing Pains*,
My problem is my legs. For 10 months, my legs have been covered in mosquito bites. I go to school and everybody says that I have got AIDS. And even when I go out, they say that I have got some disease. I am completely covered in them. I don't go out anymore. I am frightened. I'm only 12 but when I'm about 16 I will want to go out with boys and I will be covered in scars. I've tried all types of creams but none of them work and the bites are gradually spreading up to my face. Please help me.

You haven't got AIDS and you haven't got acne spots but you *probably do have a cat*. You see, mosquitoes don't really flourish all the year round (part of the time they actually live under water and don't bite anyone). But now that people have well-heated homes all the year round, the *fleas* on their *cats* flourish, and they specialise in feeding on legs. So I suggest you buy your pussy a flea-collar as soon as possible and you won't get bitten again. If you don't pick the spots, the scars will quickly vanish and you'll be able to go out with boys when the right time comes along. (PS – If you wore coloured tights no one could tell anyway.)

Natalie in Somerset asks about:

Warts – I have a lot of them on my hands and have tried many ways of getting rid of them including Compound W, but nothing seems to work. Have you got any ideas?

Yes, ask your GP if he or she does 'Cryosurgery' or knows where you can get it. This is a freezing technique which dries the wart up at once, leaving a crust to fall away in due course. It is painless.

Finally in this section, E writes from Banbury:

Dear Superlot,
I have a great deal of hair on my upper lip and people are always making jokes and remarks about the bearded lady and suchlike. Is there anything that can disguise it? I've heard that you can bleach it – is this true?

Yes, bleaching is fine but be careful. The bleach you use is *not* the stuff that Mum or Dad stick down the sink or toilet. Ask the chemist for bleach for 'facial hair' or you will give yourself a nasty burn.

CHAPTER 9

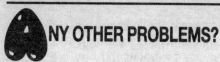 # NY OTHER PROBLEMS?

From what to do about big feet, to how to control your temper. This section includes all those questions that don't fall into any obvious general category but still need answering.

AIDS

Frances from London asks:

Please can you help me? Is it possible to get AIDS from having your ears pierced?

Six weeks ago I persuaded my mother to have her ears pierced. This was done at a big store in Bond Street. Everything was fine and she had no bleeding or infection. They used the 'gun' method. Later, a friend told me that she shouldn't have had it done, as it is a way of catching AIDS.

On Friday, her six weeks were up and she could take out her sleepers. She was practising taking them out and putting them in. She had a bit of difficulty with this, as she has arthritis, so I was helping her. She made her ear bleed a little and when I was putting the butterfly on her new earring the spike of the earring stuck in my finger and drew blood.

Please, Phillip, is it possible for her to have got AIDS? Is it possible for me to have caught it? My Mum says I'm nuts and always have to have something to worry about. I am 16½.

AIDS is caused by a virus – a bug – which is really pretty puny, and actually very difficult to catch. It can be killed by air, by hot water, by bleach, by detergent, by steam and by other chemicals. It is only dangerous if it gets inside your body and it is not nearly so good at doing this as other viruses (such as the virus that causes 'flu).

Ear-piercing carries almost no risk of giving you *any* AIDS-type virus because:

○ the virus dies outside the body
○ the equipment in any major shop would be sterilised
○ few people have actually got AIDS, although it is a growing problem.

If you are really worried, your doctor can arrange for you to be checked but I guess your Mum is right. You are a bit of a worrier anyway and maybe you would like to tackle that problem instead? Write a list of all the things that make you anxious. List all the 'bad' and 'frightening' experiences that ever happened to you as a young child. Admit to yourself how frightened you have been. Try and reach inside yourself to find the panic and the anger you must have experienced. Then try to share that with a good and close friend so that you start to feel entitled to your fears as they happen, giving them some attention instead of pushing them away. At the moment, your anxieties tend to 'leak out' when you don't want them to, don't they?

BIG FEET

Her feet are a problem for Andrea in Lincoln:

I have a personal problem which you will probably laugh at

and think I am over-reacting to, but it matters very deeply to me.

The thing is, I take size 14 shoes and I would like to know if it's possible to have an operation to cut part of my toes off. I would be very grateful if you could let me have some information as to whom I should contact. I realise I would have to pay to have this done and that it would not be cheap, but the money is not the problem.

Please take this letter seriously, as it is a serious cry for help. People close to me tell me I have to learn to live with this but I can't. I am 25 and the older I get the more it bothers me. You could never understand how depressed I get about it but I do.

You seem to think people won't understand what you are going through and I wonder whether this is also a problem you have – feeling that people don't give you any support or sympathy? If they don't, of course, it must make it much harder for you to bear your difficulties. It also means that trying to find a good friend might be even more important than thinking no one could like you on account of your physical size.

You cannot have an operation to reduce the size of your feet because there is nothing wrong with them medically. Moreover, you need your toes for balance and lift. If they were 'cut', you'd find walking difficult and probably fall over.

I think you should realise that you are very depressed about this and need help with that too. Write to MIND, 22 Harley Street, London W1, enclosing a stamped addressed envelope, and ask for their leaflet on how to tackle depression. If it helps, you can order hand-made shoes in any size from Design Studio, Longwater Industrial Estate, Dereham Road, Norwich, NR5 0TL, or Adams and Jones, Crispin Hall, High Street, Glastonbury, Somerset.

CRUSHES

Laura in Cirencester is in love:

I hope you can help me with a problem that is really worrying me. I am 14 and I have a crush on a female teacher at school. She is my form teacher.

I don't feel sexually attracted to her exactly, but I just admire her and her clothes etc. I find myself thinking about her a lot and sometimes I imagine she is watching everything that I do. She teaches numerous subjects including sex education. I feel very close to her and feel that I'd be able to talk to her about any problems, but I can't tell her about this, I really can't. I think it all started a few months ago when she was talking to us about sanitary protection in registration (I am not in any of her lessons). There is a possibility that I might be leaving my school this term and I'm worried about how I'll feel if I do leave.

There is nobody who I can talk to about this. I can't tell my mother – she thinks homosexuality is unnatural. Does all this mean I am a lesbian?

Love and sex are *not* the same thing. We can fall in love with and have a 'crush' on literally anyone. It doesn't mean we're this or that, sexually speaking. It's just a form of attraction and longing and passion. You feel tremendous tender admiration for your teacher and there's nothing 'wrong' with that at all.

I could explain some of the reasons *why* it happens to you like this – but let me stress that the feeling itself is real. In some ways, you don't feel able to confide in your parents or anyone else. You feel isolated. This woman has talked to you about 'difficult' matters and you have therefore focused your longing to be understood on to her. You are also going through a stage where you have to become a person with an identity separate from that of your Mum and the other women in your family. So you are looking around for models – your teacher is the sort of person you would like to be. She has the kind of image you admire.

There's no need to tell her what you are feeling – she probably guesses some of it anyway. It's quite normal for girls in school (boys too) to have these experiences. It will hurt when you have to leave her class but this feeling isn't all bad. It shows you that you can be loving towards someone and feel sad when you leave them. It makes you open to forming friendships, and more will come along, not always with such an age gap and not always with your own sex. It may help to open up more with your parents as well. Or to another adult or teacher.

Indeed, that's what Eleanor from Morpeth did:

I'm writing to you about something that people seem to ignore – the issue of having a crush on a teacher of the same sex. I'm a girl of 15 and at the moment I've got a crush on a female teacher. It was frightening at first because I had no one to turn to – no help, no advice. I told one of my close friends. Then I told another. I wanted to know what to do. I wanted to tell the teacher, and part of me still does. But then I decided to go for advice to *another* teacher. She understood and sat down with me and talked to me like an adult. So you shouldn't be afraid or embarrassed to confide in someone else, it really can help.

DANDRUFF

A worried Edinburgh viewer writes:

I have a growing problem. Dandruff! I have been using the 'Leading Anti-Dandruff Shampoo' (as they say on TV) since November and, generally, it seemed to keep dandruff away but in the last couple of months the problem has got worse. Please help me and advise what to do.

Dandruff is a nuisance but *not* a health hazard. It simply means that you are producing small flakes of dead skin on your scalp which float down like an embarrassing snowstorm. I suspect you have been shampooing *too* frequently with your leading shampoo and actually helping to cause the problem, by giving your scalp no rest from the strong chemical base in the lotion. Try using the dandruff shampoo just once weekly and a mild shampoo or even a baby shampoo for any in-between washes. If this doesn't work after 6 weeks, you could ask your GP for further help.

FEET AGAIN

Ben in Kingsway writes:

I feel very silly but my problem is that my feet are different sizes. Am I the freak of London? It's very expensive buying shoes.

No, you're definitely not a freak. Lots of people have this trouble and few of us have a pair of feet which could be called a perfect match. Clark's Shoes run an 'odd-size' scheme – ask at any stockist. There's also a good independent scheme to put people in touch with each other so that they can swap the shoes they don't want when they buy a new pair of ordinary-sized shoes – if you think this would help, contact Mrs Pearce, 9 Lawford Grove, Solihull B90 1EX.

LEGS

Wendy in Northern Ireland is afraid that she's lame:

I'm a very worried girl. My problem is that there is something wrong with my legs. I don't know if you can help me but I hope so. I think I've had it from when I was either 6 or 7. I can't move my legs, and my brother has it too. He calls it crippled legs. If I have to go and answer the door after sitting still for a while, I can hardly move. I hate doing PE sometimes. Especially in the summer when you have to practise for sports day.

Very simply, Wendy, I think you are sitting on your legs. This stops the blood from flowing quickly enough to keep the muscles working. When you stand up, you have cramp. Then you probably get 'pins and needles' as the feeling comes back, and then you can move again. It happens to all of us sometimes. When I sleep on my tummy with my head on my arms I occasionally wake up and am completely unable to move my arms. This means I can only turn over by twisting over in bed using my legs and tummy muscles until the 'circulation' in my arms returns. I am told it looks very funny.

Try not to sit with your legs under you, one leg tucked beneath the other or with legs crossed at all because it is bad for you anyway. (PS – I don't think this has anything to do with PE!)

LISPING

This problem concerns X from Gateshead:

Please help. I am 13 and I have got a lisp. I cannot pronounce words with the letter 's' in them. I can put up with it when I'm with people I know but when I am walking down the street talking to a friend and some boys or girls start laughing at me, it really gets to me.
(PS – My Dad says I will grow out of it. Will I?)

Lisping means making the sound 'th' instead of 's'. There are various reasons for it – the most common one is trouble with your front teeth. If you have a biggish gap between your front teeth, you cannot press your tongue into quite the right position to make the 's' sound. Or it could be that you put the tip of your tongue between your teeth, not realising that it has to be placed further inside the mouth and shouldn't actually touch the teeth at all. The more you stick your tongue out, the more the sound becomes 'th'.

Ask your dentist for advice. If your teeth need braces, you can find out the best age to get these and whether or not they will help you to say words like 'sausages' properly.

SLEEP PROBLEMS

Serena in Blackpool writes:

Dear 'Agony Uncle',
I am writing on behalf of my 16-year-old friend. She just cannot get to sleep at night. She's tried changing ends but that still doesn't work. Can you suggest some ways to me, so that I can pass them on to her, as her exams are coming up and she is worrying like mad?

Well, the reason for your friend's insomnia is no mystery – she is anxious and bothered about her exams. This is a kind of stress and it keeps the brain awake. First, tell her that losing a bit of sleep is harmless. Get her to accept that at times of higher stress like this, her sleep will probably be more disturbed. If she worries about not sleeping this will *also* prevent her from sleeping.

Second, unless we get daily exercise our bodies don't feel ready to sleep at night. When revising for exams, a lot of people stay indoors and don't walk or run at all. This is not wise, so make sure she has a daily physical as well as mental work-out.

Third, don't study until late at night because it will only take you longer to calm down and feel ready for bed. We need to go through a 'play' period to change rhythms before we can switch from being alert to feeling drowsy.

Fourth, eat a good balanced diet. Don't live on black coffee (which keeps you awake) or pep pills. Drink fruit juice when your anxiety makes you thirsty, as it will.

Fifth, when you find you cannot fall asleep at bedtime, don't lie there thrashing about. Get up, drink a cup of herbal tea or something milky if that helps. Have a bath if you can and do something routine, like sewing on a button or cutting your fingernails. I find it's a great help to play patience when I feel like this.

All this should take about half an hour, and by then you will probably be ready to drop. If not, give yourself a break for a little longer. Relaxation exercises are also helpful (see the end of the chapter on Fears and phobias).

SMOKING

This letter comes from a girl aged 14, who would prefer to remain unnamed:

When I was 11 years old, I started at a comprehensive school. I also started to smoke. I am now 14 and I have just about managed to kick the habit. But now I am thinking of starting again because I am going through a lot of pain. My back aches and my muscles hurt but nothing hurt when I smoked.

Do not tell me to go to the doctor's, as I can't speak to a man about this problem. My mother and father do not know I used to smoke either. I know you will tell me not to start again but you wouldn't like to go through it. Please tell me what this pain is, if you know.

I would like you to tell other children what I had to go through. If they do smoke and want to give up the habit but say they can't, all they need is willpower. I gave up by willpower and having a hobby. Something to keep you busy is also very important.

I am not going to tell you to do anything. I would simply point out that smoking again will not stop your back from hurting. There seems little point in giving yourself two problems instead of one, or did I miss something?

Just because your back didn't hurt when you smoked doesn't prove that giving up cigarettes has caused the pain. I don't know why your back is troubling you. There are dozens of reasons why it could be damaged – from simply bending down too much, to something quite serious. But I do know that it should be checked by a doctor soon. If you want to see a woman GP, ask if this is possible at the surgery. You only have to speak to the receptionist (even on the telephone). Lots of surgeries have several doctors working there, and more in the holidays.

Giving up smoking is the single most important thing you could ever do for your health. Willpower is OK for some. For others, writing out a contract with a friend to give up together, using chewing gum, being prepared for the moments you know will make you want to smoke again, learning how to distract yourself when they come, and saying, 'The craving to smoke only lasts a few weeks and the craving for each ciggy only lasts for a few seconds' are also techniques that help.

STAMMERING

Brian in Liverpool says:

I am 12½ years old. I have had a stammer for a few years now though it's not as bad as it used to be. When I try to say a word beginning with 'd', I usually can't get any of the word out, not even the 'd'. I usually have a stammer on words beginning with 'm', 'n' or 'l' and also other letters. People sometimes laugh at me and it's embarrassing – especially when I can't get a word out and I have to change the word. I hate reading in class or being in plays. Mum says it will go but when it does, if it does, it will be too late.

I know you feel desperate sometimes, but you've already made progress by writing to *Growing Pains*. And there's such a lot more you can do:

● The single most helpful thing you can do is consciously speak more slowly. Resist that pressure inside you to speed up. It doesn't matter if people are kept waiting a bit. They will actually listen to you more, since you're in charge of the conversation at that point.

- Please don't avoid words or try to hide your stammer. It only gives your mind more to cope with at a time when it needs to be uncluttered.
- Pause between sentences, even between words, so that you can command your audience's attention.
- Make eye-contact with the person you are talking to. Half the battle is winning more self-confidence in social settings, and conversation is the most common form of social contact between people.
- Do 'mirror work'. Look at what you do when you stammer so that you can see what you have to change – whether it's a certain expression that makes you stumble or whatever.
- Practise reading aloud to yourself with a pair of headphones playing music in your ears so that you 'mask' your own voice. And with those difficult 'd's, try making a lighter contact between your tongue and the top of the back of your teeth. Keep saying 'dum-diddy' to yourself as part of your practice.

For further help, contact the Association of Stammerers, 86 Blackfriars Road, London SE1 8HA.

TEMPER

Helen in South Wales simply says:

Dear Uncle Agony,

I know this is a stupid problem. But can you tell me how to keep my temper? I've counted up to 10. It didn't work. I've tried to ignore everyone. And that didn't work. Please help me. I would be so grateful if you did.

So, biting your feelings back has failed, has it? It usually does. The trouble with anger (of which temper is a part) is that it's a normal and necessary feeling. Unfortunately, some people disapprove of it. They can't stand any rows, or shouting or defiance or rebellion. Hard luck to them. People need to sound off at times.

And that's the solution to your problem. Give yourself permission to get irritated about the everyday things which annoy you as they arise. That way you won't build up such a big head of steam that you *have* to explode when somebody says or does the wrong thing. Speak up for yourself more. It's not evil to be tetchy. Just remember – if you let out the little irritations, you won't explode in a huge outburst of temper.

THUMB-SUCKING

This letter comes from Bronwen in Cardiff:

I am now 16 years old. My problem is that I still suck my thumb. I only do this after school if I'm tired, and it helps me sleep at night. My parents hate me doing it and I think they are beginning to think there's something wrong with me.

I know many people in my year who suck their thumbs at school in front of everyone, which I would never do. I would like to stop sucking my thumb but I like doing it a lot. I've tried to stop many times without success. Once, in a doctor's magazine I read that adults who sucked their thumbs were mentally ill. Is this true? Should I go to the doctor's? I hope not. Please could you tell me how to stop and why I do it.

We suck our thumbs for comfort, just as we once

sucked on our mother's breast, or on a 'cuddle-cloth' or a baby's bottle. It's both an instinctive pleasure and a habit. Adults who do it are perfectly sane, but they often have feelings of anxiety or sadness and a longing to try and return to their childhood. I wonder if you ever feel like this?

Your parents hate your habit because they worry that you will not grow up normally and become an independent adult. I should try to understand their point of view but also make them aware that it would help you give up your thumb if they were a bit more affectionate. A little more comfort at night, a kiss in the morning and maybe a hug when you come home – these are some of the things you probably need.

I am not making suggestions when I say this, but you will probably feel less like sucking your thumb when you start going out with boys and feel that someone really cares for you and stands by you. You are doing yourself no medical damage whatsoever (though you should try not to pull your teeth forward).

WAYS OUT

Finally, in this section we hear from Alexander in Hampstead, aged 7. He explains how to solve your basic problem:

How do you get out of a room with only a table in it and no exits?

You scream till you get a sore throat, take the saw and cut the table in half, two halves make a hole and you crawl through the hole . . .

And thank you too.